LENIN

Notes for a Biographer

Leon Trotsky

LENIN
Notes for a Biographer

WITH AN INTRODUCTION BY BERTRAM D. WOLFE

*Translated from the Russian and annotated
by Tamara Deutscher*

CAPRICORN BOOKS
NEW YORK

Contents

Introduction

I

THIS BOOK differs greatly from Trotsky's other writings. It was written hurriedly because Lenin had just died, because the Communist Party and all Russia were confronted by the disconcerting questions: *Who next? What next?* It was rushed to the press because Stalin had cunningly deceived Trotsky about the day of Lenin's burial to convince the ailing Trotsky that he could not possibly arrive from a sanitarium in the Caucasus in time for the funeral. All of Lenin's close associates would say their last words and march in the final procession with the coffin of the fallen leader, save only the one who from 1917 on had been most nearly Lenin's equal. Not to be an honorary pallbearer, nor watch at the coffin, nor speak a solemn farewell, nor march with the rest of Lenin's close companions, was of enormous moral significance in the eyes of the sorrowing party members, and of no less political significance in a still muted struggle for the succession that had begun even while Lenin lay dying. This was going on during that last year when Lenin was made helpless by a third stroke that paralyzed both tongue and pen. Trotsky's *Lenin* was rushed into print without the author's customary fastidious attention to style and structure because the whole country expected a "last word" from the man who would undoubtedly have received more votes in the party and the country for Lenin's post than all of Lenin's other close associates combined, had a popular vote been permitted at that moment.

Trotsky prided himself on his Russian style, and not without reason. For his underground name he chose *Pero,* the Russian word for "pen." But though unaccustomed to modesty concerning his writings, he modestly subtitled the present work *Notes for a Biographer.* Twice he calls the work "unfinished," and, concerning the first section dealing with his youthful, admiring contact with the older Lenin, whom he regarded for a while as an oracle, he adds in unwonted surprise: "I see all the inadequacy in the episodes recounted by me above; they have turned out more impoverished than I had expected when I started this work." (Of course, when he comes to the year 1917 and Trotsky and Lenin join hands in a common cause, the "impoverishment" of which Trotsky speaks disappears.)

If in the latter part, almost four-fifths of the book, the excitement and interest increase and the revelations are both intimate and illuminating, still there is a larger sense in which these *Notes for a Biographer* may properly be said to be "unfinished." They are unfinished because they were written when Trotsky was ill with malaria; because Lenin was but three months dead and the ailing Trotsky had had no time for research and reflection; because he had not yet figured out how he should handle the more than thirteen years of estrangement between Lenin and himself; and because his factional opponents were using exclusively the sharp epithets he and Lenin had aimed at each other during that period to make it seem that Trotsky had always been an anti-Leninist and an anti-Bolshevik, while deliberately suppressing the eventful years from 1917 on when Lenin and Trotsky fought shoulder to shoulder. The *Notes for a Biographer* are unfinished in a literal sense too, for as Trotsky hints, he hoped himself to be that biographer for whom these first hurried notes were written. Indeed he was to begin a life of Lenin in the thirties when he was living in exile, driven from land to land by the diplomatic and extra-diplomatic pressures of the government he had done so much to bring into being. He brought to completion one remarkable slender volume to serve as Part I. It was written in Russian as *Lenin, Junost (Lenin, Youth)*, but there was no way for him to get it published in his native tongue, much less his native land. After his assassination, people who admired the manuscript brought it out in an excellent German and a no less excellent French translation as *Der junge Lenin* and *La Jeunesse de Lénine*. There is no way of knowing whether he would have kept up the high level of writing in a later, more partisan account of Lenin as politician and conspiratorial revolutionary, but this first part remains the best account of Lenin's childhood and youth that has been written in any language.

The reason why the Lenin biography remained unfinished was that Trotsky gave, as is understandable, greater priority to a critique of Stalin's deeds, to the defense of his own reputation and that of the victims of the purge trials against Stalin's slander machine, and to a biography of Stalin. Like the biography of Lenin, the life of Stalin remained unfinished. He had completed five chapters and a number of notes and short runs for the remaining chapters of the book, and was working in his study in Coyoacán, Mexico, on the manuscript, when one of Stalin's professional killers gained access to his beleaguered semifortress on the pretext that he wanted Trotsky's judgment on an article the secret agent had prepared on French politics. While Trotsky was bending over the manuscript, the visitor buried an Alpine pick in his brain, his blood running appropriately over a page of the manuscript dedicated to the bloody tyrant. An editor, Charles Malamuth, working from the notes and runs of intended text, finished the work as best he could, and it has appeared as *Stalin, An Appraisal of the Man and His Influence.* Thus, both biographies remain unfinished.

II

Despite Trotsky's modesty concerning the "inadequacy" and the "impoverishment" of the first section of his book, it is of considerable interest to us because it gives the fresh impressions of a twenty-three-year-old admiring youth concerning the founder and leader of Bolshevism, who was approximately a decade older and already respectfully referred to by his followers as "the Old Man."

On their first encounter, Lenin casually conducted him through the streets of London, more interested in giving the young disciple a searching examination than in showing him the sights. Occasionally the guide interrupts his cross-examination on what Trotsky has read, the opinions he has formed, how he estimates certain factional competitors, by pointing to a building and saying, "This is *their* Westminster, *their* London *Times,* or *their* British Museum." There was a certain inflection in Lenin's voice when he pronounced the word "their," Trotsky writes, that "meant of course not belonging to the English but belonging to the enemy. . . . In his eyes the shadow of the exploiting classes lay over the whole of human culture and this shadow was as visible to him as the light of day." Manifestly a man who could say *"their* Westminster" in that tone was not one who thought much of Parliamentarism or the "Mother of Parliaments." And one who thus said *"their* London *Times"* would be more likely to produce a propaganda journal than a source of world news coverage and information. Even the British Museum, where Marx researched for and wrote *Das Kapital,* would not escape the same faintly derogatory intonation of the word "their." Over all the monuments of culture and democracy lay "the shadow as visible as the light of day."

From the examination which Lenin gave his young disciple as they walked through the great city, one gets the feeling that Lenin lived only physically in London, but his spirit was immersed wholly in the factional and doctrinal controversies of Russia. Unwittingly Trotsky gives the same picture of himself. Here is a young provincial Russian abroad in the fabled and much discussed West, but instead of being as excited as all intellectual travelers from Russia were in the nineteenth century, he writes, "I took in Vienna, Paris, and London in a rather summary fashion and could hardly take notice of such 'details' as Westminster castle." Lenin did not even point out to him that there were two "castles," a Parliament building and an abbey, or if he did, the young sightseer took no notice. This indifference to Western Europe and its institutions and values so exalted or so denigrated by most Russian intellectuals remained with both men all their lives. They lived in the West for long periods out of necessity, but were in it not part of it, for wherever they went they carried a bit of Russia with them like a nimbus around their heads, which helps to explain the mistakes both men made in their judgments of Western Europe whether in power in Russia or living in exile in some West European land.

This first section of Trotsky's *Lenin* gives us tantalizingly brief but fascinating pen-portraits of the other editors of *Iskra*: the haughty and learned Marxist, Plekhanov, Lenin's master and first teacher, already being challenged by the disciple for the leadership of the *Iskra* group; the wise and modest Axelrod who knew so much about trade unions, non-Party mass movements, and socialist organization principles; and above all, the attractive, somewhat bohemian Vera Zasulich, who knew the peasant best, understood more than all the others the land question, and possessed the deepest and most ample human, in contradistinction to class, feelings. Both Lenin and Trotsky comment slightingly on the fact that her opposition to autocracy and abject poverty was based "more on moral-political foundations" than on a mastery of the fine points of Russian orthodox Marxist formulas and dogmas. "With Vera Ivanovna," Lenin told his young disciple condescendingly, "too much is based on morality, on feelings."

Vera Ivanovna Zasulich had acquired fame as a young girl when she shot General Trepov because he ordered the knout to be used on political prisoners. The public approved, a jury acquitted her, and an underground organization facilitated her escape abroad. Once when Lenin, the *de facto* editor of *Iskra,* was away, Zasulich and Martov brought out an issue of the paper. It contained news that the Governor of Vilna had ordered demonstrating working men flogged, and this awakened the old spirit in Vera Zasulich. When Lenin saw her feelings about floggings and the desirability of punitive terror expressed in the columns of *Iskra,* he was indignant not so much at the governor as at the two editors for "taking the first step on the road to capitulation to the Social Revolutionaries" who based their movement more on morality than on "science" and were more given to individual terror as a curb to official cruelty than were the Marxists.

However fragmentary, such details are precious for the light they shed on Lenin. And significantly, in all the differences between Vera Ivanovna and Lenin which Trotsky reveals with a touch of condescension, she comes out best in the end.

Thus Lenin was inclined to revere the German Social Democratic Party as the model party of the International, and denounced one of his close followers as "an idiot" for doubting the revolutionary temper of Karl Kautsky. Zasulich, however, calmly declared that a party that had learned "to live with their Kaiser" was not to be trusted to make a revolution. A scarce decade later, Lenin would be denouncing the German Social Democrats as traitors, writing a pamphlet on *The*

Proletarian Revolution and the Renegade Kautsky, and denouncing Karl Kautsky as "the most dangerous of all."

Similarly, Trotsky reveals Lenin and Zasulich as quarreling over the distribution of the land to the peasants. She was in favor of distributing all the remaining land while Lenin dogmatically insisted that a proper agrarian program required only the distribution of the *otrezki* (the "cut off portions"), the tiny parcels which the gentry had been authorized to cut off from the peasant-tilled lands when those lands were distributed in the Emancipation of 1861. Averaged over the country, Lenin's modest demand would equal only 4.1 hectares per farm. Again her land distribution program seemed to Lenin a "capitulation to the Social Revolutionaries," but in his first land decree of 1917 he took over wholesale the land distribution she had been advocating, "plagiarizing it," as he himself wrote, "from the Social Revolutionaries."

Finally, we cannot help but wonder whether, if Lenin had had more of Vera Zasulich's moral feelings concerning human beings as human beings and not mere adjuncts of classes, the regime he installed might not have been a gentler one exacting less cost in human lives and human freedom.

It is such insights, many of which have not come to us from any other source, that make this first brief section of Trotsky's memories of Lenin so interesting to the contemporary reader and to the students of this history-making man's life and thought.

III

Trotsky's first contact with Lenin as a worshipful disciple lasted only some eleven months, from October, 1902, when Lenin was grooming him for the editorial board of *Iskra,* to some time in August, 1903, at the Second Congress of the Social Democratic Party, when Trotsky, along with four of the *Iskra* editors and other socialist leaders opened a blistering attack on Lenin's authoritarianism, his extreme centralism, his attempt to establish a "state of siege" and a personal dictatorship in the party. The attacks of Leon Trotsky and Rosa Luxemburg, neither of them on the *Iskra* board, were the most powerful and cutting, and Lenin felt them most keenly. Particularly for his youthful ex-disciple, Lenin had only words of scorn and ridicule, epithets which now during Lenin's last paralyzed silence and after his death Trotsky's opponents in the struggle for the Leninist succession were using unmercifully to "prove" that Trotsky had always been an anti-Leninist and an anti-Bolshevik. It is on these thirteen years of bitter epithets and controversies that Trotsky has nothing to say in the present work, a silence that was to prove embarrassing and hurtful. And indeed it is embarrassing that these *Notes for a Biographer* have not one word to say of Lenin between August, 1903, and April, 1917, when the two men joined forces in a fruitful and successful partnership.

Naturally, during the thirteen years in which they fought each other, they engaged in much justified and unjustified polemical abuse. They said many things of each other that both men were glad to forget during their close association from 1917 until paralysis ended Lenin's activity.

In the stormy year 1905 the two men were close to each other, just as they were during the storms of 1917. In 1905 Lenin was startled to find that the masses were capable of huge unimaginable initiatives without the direction of his party. He hailed their march to the palace to petition the czar, though the march was led by a priest and the marchers bore ikons of saints and of the emperor. He celebrated their initiative in the vast succession of strikes that followed, their defiant seizure of the rights of freedom of speech, assembly, and organization, and their great general strike of October, 1905, for which Leon Trotsky was the people's tribune and spokesman. At first Lenin opposed the Soviets founded on the initiative of the working men because the Soviets were not Bolshevik-constituted, Bolshevik-infiltrated and -dominated nor Bolshevik-led. But after the Soviets led the great October General Strike, he hailed them as the leaders of the strike and "the germ of a provisional revolutionary government" (in a letter to *Novaya Zhizn* written in November, 1905, but suppressed by the Bolshevik censorship until its publication in *Pravda* on November 5, 1940). At the time this was written Leon Trotsky was the *de facto* Chairman of the Soviet Congress.

Overwhelmed by the revolutionary inventiveness of the masses, Lenin dropped for a year his insistence on party direction and authoritarian centralism, and even his inveterate splitting habits so that Trotsky had no reason to continue his polemics against Lenin. Besides he was much too busy as the leading figure in the Soviet. As for the Bolshevik attacks on Trotsky in November, 1905, they gave way to praise. When the first issue of the Menshevik daily, *Nachalo,* was brought out under the editorship of Trotsky and Parvus, Lenin's *Novaya Zhizn* wrote: "We welcome a comrade in the struggle. The first issue is notable for the brilliant description of the October strife written by Comrade Trotsky." And when Trotsky replaced the inept lawyer Khrustalev as "strong man of the Soviet," Lenin told Lunacharsky, "Well, Trotsky has won this by his tireless and striking work." Had Trotsky had time to reflect before he wrote his *Notes for a Biographer* he would surely have treated this rapprochement with Lenin in 1905 as a preview of their partnership of 1917.

In omitting to give an account of the thirteen years of controversy between himself and Lenin, Trotsky omitted much that was trivial and transient, for the logic of factional strife drove both contenders to inflate many petty and unimportant things. But during this period, which Trotsky here covers with silence, each of them raised against the other one large issue that was to be of fundamental significance to the whole future of the Bolshevik Party and the regime it was to inaugurate in November, 1917. Had Trotsky stuck to that criticism of Lenin and Lenin to his comparable criticism of Trotsky, the Communist regime might have been less harsh and Trotsky's closing years less tragic.

Long after Lenin's death, Trotsky was to write concerning Lenin's successor: "Stalin represents a phenomenon utterly exceptional. He is neither a thinker, nor a writer, nor an orator. He took possession of power not with the aid of personal qualities but with the aid of an impersonal machine. And it was not he who created the machine, but the machine that created him."

Inevitably, the question arises in our minds: What machine? Who created that machine and put his stamp upon it? What was there in the nature of that machine that could create a Stalin, permit him to vault so easily into the driver's seat, and drive the juggernaut over the bodies of all of Lenin's closest associates, over Trotsky himself, over the party, the peasantry, the working men, the managers, the party ideologists, and the officers in the Russian Army? Neither in the present work nor anywhere in his later writings does Trotsky ask and answer that question.

Yet there was a time, back in the year 1904, when Trotsky rose to the heights of analytical prevision to forewarn Lenin that the machine he was creating would breed personal dictatorship. "The organization of the party," he wrote prophetically, "will take the place of the party itself; the Central Committee will take the place of the organization; and finally the dictator will take the place of the Central Committee." A true and fateful prophecy, for this tendency was indeed inherent in Lenin's machine, with its authoritarianism, its supercentralism, its infallible doctrine requiring a single interpretation and a single infallible interpreter—lest pluralism reappear in the insidious form of multiple and contending interpretations. Such a machine could more readily elevate a machine man to power than it could a "thinker, writer, and orator." The General Secretary could appoint and control the local secretaries and select his supporters as delegates to a congress. Trotsky could only have had a fighting chance had he fought this machine aspect of Leninism, for this was the "impersonal machine" that elevated Stalin to power over the party and the country. By accepting this machine that he had once criticized so accurately, Trotsky was choosing to fight Stalin on Stalin's battleground, and was thereby doomed to impotence and defeat. In this regard Stalin was the better Leninist, raising Lenin's machine to new heights and completing the fulfillment of Trotsky's prophetic vision of 1904. Of all of Trotsky's pronouncements there is none more pathetic than his statement of surrender to the Stalinist machine that had just rolled over him:

"None of us can be right against the party. In the last instance, the party is always right. . . . One ought not be right against the party." When Trotsky pronounced these words at a party Congress of Stalin-selected delegates, his supporters trembled and the Congress jeered, for the Congress was Stalin's while the one who would henceforth be "always right" and who incarnated in his person the party, was Joseph Stalin.

IV

As Trotsky criticized Lenin in 1904 for his theory of an undemocratic party, so Lenin criticized Trotsky in 1905 for developing a theory of an undemocratic revolution. Trotsky called his theory the doctrine of "permanent revolution." Lenin's criticism was gentler than was his wont, for he made it at a time when he was being compelled to admiration of Trotsky for his leading role in the Petrograd Soviet and the October General Strike. Moreover, there was an ambiguity in Lenin's own spirit which secretly inclined him to accept Trotsky's thesis.

Lenin always regarded himself as an orthodox Marxist, and orthodox Russian Marxism, particularly as taught by his master Plekhanov, held that Russia was too backward for a socialist revolution, its proletariat too unorganized, too inexperienced, too uncultured, and in numbers only a tiny island in a surrounding peasant sea. What Russia was facing, the Marxists held, was a "bourgeois democratic revolution." The duty of the party of the proletariat was to fight for "bourgeois democracy" and help the bourgeoisie to come to power. I must leave it to the reader to decide whether they are flattering the bourgeoisie or belittling democracy and civil liberties by calling them bourgeois, but in any case the bourgeoisie was supposed to introduce a democratic republic, universal suffrage, freedom to organize, and thus enable the proletariat to mature and prepare its own socialist revolution. Without such democracy, Plekhanov warned, the overthrow of a particular autocrat would be followed by a restoration of autocracy. Even worse, it might perhaps be a restoration of a more autocratic despotism on a pseudosocialist basis. If, as Lenin was to propose in 1907, the revolutionary government should nationalize the land, this would only tighten the bonds that bound the peasantry to the state, and produce a new ruling caste like the "Inca sons of the sun." With his head Lenin accepted this orthodox teaching of his master, but in his heart there was ambivalence, for the idea of helping the bourgeoisie to power and postponing the struggle of his own party for power until he was perhaps long dead, went against his ardent, power-concentrated temperament. Hence he looked long and wistfully at Trotsky's view that the bourgeoisie would be too weak and cowardly in Russia to fight for its own "bourgeois democratic revolution," and too afraid of the concentrated, fighting proletariat to install democratic freedoms. The English revolution of the sixteenth century, Trotsky argued, still had to be fought "in a religious guise." But the French Revolution at the end of the seventeenth century "could dispense with religion." Now it was the twentieth century, and, just as Russia was borrowing the latest technology from abroad, so it could borrow the latest political technology, that of socialist revolution. The proletariat itself would have to take power and, once in power, could "leap over democracy" and at once begin its advance toward socialism. Moreover, its revolutionary example would stir the socialist proletariat of Western Europe to take power, and they would help the Russian workers overcome their backwardness.

Very clever, Lenin thought, and devilishly tempting, yet, remembering the pronouncements of Marx and Engels on Russia and Plekhanov's solemn warning, he refused to be tempted. Moreover, he did not yet feel himself so near to power that he could imagine what it would be like to renounce one's own revolution and hand power over to the bourgeoisie, so, much as he felt the attraction of Trotsky's activist thesis, he nevertheless uttered a grave and, as it turned out, a prophetic warning against Trotsky's proposal to "leap over democracy" and keep the revolution going in permanence until it brought about international and Russian socialism.

"Whoever attempts to achieve socialism," he warned, "by any other route than that of political democracy, will inevitably arrive at the most absurd and reactionary results, both political and economic." And in 1917, this, too, proved to be a true prophecy. For in that fateful year when he and Trotsky joined forces, they amnestied each other's cardinal errors. Trotsky accepted Lenin's undemocratic machine. Lenin accepted Trotsky's undemocratic revolution with its "leap over democracy." An undemocratic party to make an undemocratic revolution—what are these if not the very foundations of totalitarianism?

After the eleven months of meager youthful memories of the *Iskra* period and the thirteen years of embarrassed silence concerning his polemics with Lenin, these memories suddenly become rich and illuminating in circumstances and details. The year is 1917 and Lenin and Trotsky are joining hands in a common struggle to overthrow the democratic Provisional Government with its "capitalist ministers," and to convince or

silence most of Lenin's old Bolshevik lieutenants who lack
faith in the audacious enterprise and are quoting in routine
fashion Lenin's formulas of yesterday against his judgments
and purposes of today. We get Trotsky's picture of the Bolshevik July offensive and Lenin's decision to go into hiding
after its failure. "Now they will shoot all of us," Lenin tells
Trotsky, for that is what Lenin would have done under similar
circumstances. We get Trotsky's version of the help furnished
Lenin by the German General Staff, not the true picture but
doubtless the one that Trotsky accepted. The final proof that
Lenin received financial help as well as passage through the
German lines came into our possession only after our forces
captured the relevant German archives during the Occupation
following World War II.

There are callous, boastful, unforgettable pictures of the
cruelty of soldiers and sailors brutalized by three years of total
war, "plunging their bayonets into their officers' stomachs,"
drowning officers under the ice, flinging them overboard from
ships, deserting to return to their native villages "to set fire to
the landlord's manor" and seize what land they can without
waiting for land commissions or fair partition. Occasionally
Trotsky's metaphors overreach themselves as when he has the
Social Revolutionaries, who were still destined to get a majority in the only free elections ever held in Russia, "gnashing
their rotten teeth," but there is no mistaking Lenin's feelings
or Trotsky's as they prepare to use the war-weariness, the
brutalization, the despair, and the anarchy of factory workers
expelling their foremen, of peasants driving out their landlords, of soldiers deserting the front and using their guns and
bayonets to take what they covet from whoever seems to have
it. "Rob what has been robbed" is Lenin's slogan to egg the
masses on against the weak democratic government that prepares only against a restoration of czarism undreamed of by
the czar, but not against a coup from the left, openly preached
by Lenin and openly prepared by Trotsky in the Military Rev-

olutionary Committee of the Petrograd Council of Workers and Soldiers.

Interestingly enough, Trotsky explains effectively why Lenin insisted on making the conspirative coup in October (November new style) and not later, but fails to understand why Lenin insisted that it take place on the night of October 24 and not on October 25, the day when the Soviet was to assemble. Lenin wanted to face not merely the Constituent Assembly but also the Soviet Congress with the *fait accompli* of seizure of power by his party, and this Trotsky seems not to comprehend, and not to explain. "The party could not seize power by itself, independently of the Soviets and behind their back," he writes. Yet this is exactly what Lenin insisted upon, and without understanding him, the party, including the Chairman of the Military Revolutionary Committee, Leon Trotsky, carried out his will. The night of the twenty-fourth they seized power by occupying all the symbolic buildings from which in an over-centralized country all orders were accustomed to come. There is a precious vignette of Lenin and Trotsky lying on the floor in an adjoining room waiting to be summoned to enter the hall where the Soviet was convening, feeling dizzy with the sudden transition from hiding to avoid expected arrest to the very summit of power. *"Es schwindelt,"* Lenin says to Trotsky. ("It makes one dizzy.") Later he was to write of the seizure of power, "It was as easy as lifting up a feather."

Trotsky skips then to the Brest Litovsk negotiations with the German Army already on Russian territory, and we get the only clear and truthful account of the differences in the Central Committee between three factions, Lenin the realist standing all alone with the declaration that "We must sign the shameful treaty at once . . . The peasant, by deserting the front has voted with his feet . . . Fully armed German troops 'are on our territory and can advance, for German militarism is a beast that moves swiftly." Trotsky pictures truthfully the Central Committee majority still following Lenin's slogans of yesterday and urging a summons to the world proletariat to rise to save the Russian revolution and make a world revolution, while Trotsky urges, wrongfully as it turns out, that they should temporize, try a summons to the German and world proletariat, then sign the treaty if despite these revolutionary gestures, the German Army should prove capable of resuming its advance. Lenin proved right in his assertion that "German militarism is a beast that moves swiftly"; only after the loss of much additional territory did Lenin get his majority, including the vote of Leon Trotsky. It is such intimate accounts as this that makes Trotsky's memories of Lenin of supreme importance to the historian and to any student of Lenin's character.

The story of his determination to disperse the Constituent Assembly by force is of comparable importance. After seizing power, Lenin tried to prevent the elections or postpone them until he could outlaw all other parties, but he was outvoted by his Central Committee, and then by the people of Russia over whom he had seized power. Lenin responded by bringing in a Latvian sharpshooter regiment and the Kronstadt sailors. "We have gained power," Trotsky quotes him as saying, "and at the same time we have put ourselves in a position in which we are compelled to use military means in order to win it anew." Still he consoled himself with these fateful words: "By dispersing the Constituent Assembly, the Soviet regime in the name of the dictatorship of the proletariat, has openly and finally put an end to formal democracy. This lesson will not be forgotten." And indeed, it was not forgotten, for in the next fifty years and more that have passed, never once did the rulers of Russia submit any measure or act of theirs to a popular vote again. "The open, frank and brutal dispersal of the Constituent Assembly," Trotsky gloats, "gave formal democracy the *coup de grâce* from which it was never to recover. . . . In the end, it all turned out to the good!" It is such inside stories as these that enable us to see deeply into the mechanism of the permanent dictatorship that the Bolsheviks thus inaugurated.

And it is Trotsky's rejoicing and boasting about the future of the regime thus inaugurated that gives to the entire work its inescapably tragic character. This little book was written in 1924 when Trotsky could still boast of the abolition of freedom of the press, freedom of the word, freedom of discussion and opinion, could boast of the terror and its myriad victims. He could still persuade himself that the party, "deprived of Lenin's leadership would become more united than ever . . . reject all that might endanger the clarity of its thought, the unity of its will and its fighting capacity . . . make up for the absent genius by redoubling its collective efforts . . . that all would do this from the member of the Central Committee to the Red Army soldier." He could still sneer at Chernov who, having received the popular mandate of the great majority in the elections to the Constituent Assembly, yet refused to use force to defend that assembly, preferring tolerant and civilized discussion and democratic decision among the various wings of the socialist movement.

But as we read this little work with the hindsight of almost a half century of elapsed time, we know how badly Trotsky himself was to miss this freedom of discussion among comrades, this chance to appeal to the people, this freedom of speech and press and assembly, this right to tell the truth and have it published, this right to advance and defend one's opinions. We read his hopeful boasting with the knowledge that the party machine with Stalin in the driver's seat rolled over the Central Committee, the Congress, the party, the peasantry, the working class, the intelligentsia, and ended by depriving all of Lenin's closest companions, Trotsky included, of their rights, the record of their service, their morals, their dignity, their lives. How terrible does Trotsky's arrogant and boastful exaltation of terror become as we contemplate the long reach of Stalin to Trotsky's safe refuge in his fortress home in Mexico, as an Alpine pick crashes into his skull, and the blood from his brain spills over a sheet of his manuscript of the *Life of Stalin.* Our knowledge of the fearful outcome makes the exaltation of terror painful to read, but, as the testimony of the man who did more than any other except Lenin to secure the victory of the Bolshevik conspiracy, and a picture of Lenin and of Trotsky himself when they could not know the outcome of their deeds, these pages make compelling reading.

BERTRAM D. WOLFE

The Hoover Institution on War,
Revolution, and Peace
Stanford University
November 7, 1970

Foreword

This book is in two respects incomplete. First of all, one should look here neither for a biography of Lenin, nor for a study of his character, nor for a full survey of his views and methods of action. This volume provides only some materials, the outlines and sketches for future work—perhaps even for future work by the author of these lines. This somewhat "sketchy" approach is both inevitable and necessary. In addition to the popular biographies and more general character studies, there is now a need to set down on paper with more care and attention certain episodes, certain moments in Lenin's life and particular features of his personality as we were able to observe them with our own eyes. The greater part of this book consists of memories of two periods between which fifteen years elapsed: the last six months of the old *Iskra* period and the decisive year of the October upheaval, that is, to be more precise, the period from the middle of 1917 till autumn 1918.

This book is not complete in another and narrower sense of the word: I hope that circumstances will allow me to continue this work, to improve on it, to correct it, to make it more accurate, to expand it and add new episodes and new chapters.

Temporary withdrawal from day-to-day work, due to illness, helped me to recall much of what is related here. Later, while reading my first notes, the skein of memories began to unwind and further reminiscences unraveled new episodes which were interesting if only because they were connected with Lenin and with his life. However, this method of work has its disadvantages: The product is never finished. This is why at a certain point I decided to cut short the manuscript and to publish it in incomplete form. But, as I said before, I reserve to myself the right to continue work on this book, and it goes without saying that I should be most grateful to any and all of those who witnessed the events described if they came forward with corrections or if they brought to it some new memories. It should be said, however, that I have deliberately left out a whole range of episodes because they are still too closely connected with present-day affairs.

To the two main parts of the book which consist of reminiscences, I have added those articles, essays, and speeches (or fragments of speeches), for the purpose of giving a characterization of Lenin.

Working over these memories, I used hardly any documents referring to the period with which I have dealt. It seemed to me that as it was not my aim to present a full-scale historical narrative of any particular phase of Lenin's life, but only to give some first-hand source material, it would be better to rely on my own memory.

I had practically finished writing this book, when I read Volume XIV of Lenin's *Works* and the book on the Brest Litovsk peace by Comrade Ovsyannikov; the additions which resulted from this reading were very few indeed.

L. TROTSKY

P.S. On rereading the manuscript I noticed that in my reminiscences I refer to the city of Leningrad either as to Petrograd or to Petersburg. Some comrades give to the old Petrograd retrospectively the name Leningrad. To me this does not seem correct. Can one say, for example, that Lenin was arrested in Leningrad? It is obvious that this would sound very strange. It would be even more improbable to say: Peter I founded Leningrad. One can imagine that as years and decades go by the new name of a city, like all other proper names, will lose its vivid historical meaning. But for the time being we are still too much aware that Petrograd became Leningrad after January 21, 1924—and it could not have been so renamed earlier. And this is why I preserve the name of the city current at the time of the events I recall.

L. T.

April 21, 1924

I. Lenin and the Old *Iskra*

The split of 1903 was, so to say, an anticipation . . .
—LENIN IN 1910

THERE is no doubt that to a great, future biographer of Lenin the old *Iskra* period (1900–1903) will be of unique psychological interest, and also of considerable difficulty. It was precisely during this short time that Lenin became the Lenin he was to remain. This does not mean that he did not develop further. On the contrary. He grew in stature—and at what a rate!—until October and after; but this was really organic growth. The leap from illegality to the seizure of power on October 25, 1917, was enormous; but this was, so to say, outward, the shooting upward of a man who had already weighed and measured all it was possible to weigh and measure, while in the growth which occurred before the split at the Second Congress of the Party there was the imperceptible, and all the more fundamental inward development.

The aim of these reminiscences is to give the future biographer some materials which would throw light on this extremely memorable and significant period in the spiritual development of Vladimir Ilyich. From that time to the present moment of writing over two decades have passed, two decades crowding human memory quite exceptionally; this may give rise to certain doubts. How far is what is related here a correct presentation of past events? I must admit that I myself was prey to these doubts all through the process of writing. There exist already too many incoherent "memoirs" and inexact eyewitness accounts. When I drafted this essay, I had no documents and no reference material to hand whatsoever. I think that, on balance, this was all to the good. I had to rely on my memory only, and I hope that this gives my work more spontaneity and also makes it free from that unconscious retrospective touching-up which it is so difficult to avoid, even with the utmost self-discipline and self-criticism. Moreover, my writings will facilitate the sifting of evidence in future research which will be done with all the available files and documents dealing with the past.

In some passages I have reconstructed conversations and debates and present them in the form of a dialogue. Of course it is impossible to pretend that discussions which took place twenty-odd years ago are reproduced word for word, but in substance, I trust, I have related them faithfully and in case of a particularly lively exchange of words, literally.

As we are concerned here with materials for future biographers of Lenin, a question of paramount importance, I may be allowed to make a few remarks about certain qualities of my memory. I remember quite poorly the topography of cities and even of houses. In London, for example, more than once I lost my way in the relatively short distance which separated my lodgings from those of Lenin. For a long time I had a poor memory for faces, but in this respect I have made considerable progress. On the other hand, I have always had—and still have—an excellent memory for ideas, their flow and associations, and for discussions whose subjects are ideas.

That this assessment of my memory is not subjective I was able to verify on many occasions. Other people present with me at some debate related it with much less precision than I did, and they accepted my corrections. One should add, how-

ever, that young provincial that I was on arriving in London,
I was eager to learn and to see everything as rapidly as possible. No wonder that the talks with Lenin and other members
of the editorial board of *Iskra* engraved themselves on my
memory. Such then are the circumstances which future biographers will have to take into account in determining the
degree of trustworthiness of the recollections printed below.

I arrived in London in the autumn of 1902, I think in
October, very early in the morning. With signs and gestures I
managed to hire a cab which took me to the address written
on a piece of paper. My destination was the lodging of Vladimir Ilyich. I was taught in advance (it must have been still
in Zurich) to knock on the door a certain prescribed number
of times. As I remember, Nadezhda Konstantinovna opened
the door; I must have dragged her out of bed by my knocking.
It was very early in the morning, a man more experienced and
more accustomed to a civilized way of life would have stayed
quietly at the station an hour or two instead of knocking on
strangers' doors at the crack of dawn. But I was still full of
the excitement of my escape from Verkholensk. More or less
in the same manner I had descended on Axelrod's household
in Zurich—not at dawn, but in the middle of the night.

Vladimir Ilyich was still in bed, and his face expressed
kindness tinged with justifiable amazement. In such circumstances our first meeting and our first talk took place. Vladimir
Ilyich and Nadezhda Konstantinovna knew of me through a
letter from Clair (M. G. Kzhizhanovsky) who officially introduced me into the *Iskra* organization in Samara under the
pseudonym Pen. And that is how I was greeted: "Hey, Pen has
arrived!" . . . I was given tea, in the kitchen-dining room, I
think. In the meantime Lenin got dressed. I told them about
my escape and complained about the bad state of the *Iskra*
"frontier," [1] which was managed by a college boy, an SR[2] who

was unsympathetic to the *Iskra* group as a result of bitter
polemics which had just flared up. Besides, smugglers had
shamelessly fleeced me by raising all their tariffs and rates. I
handed over to Nadezhda Konstantinovna a modest batch of
addresses and a list of meeting points, or, to be more exact, I
informed her of the necessity of doing away with some addresses which had become valueless. On behalf of the Samara
group (Clair and others) I had visited Kharkov, Poltava, Kiev,
and practically everywhere, in any case in Kharkov and Poltava, I found that the organizational links were extremely
defective.

The same morning, or perhaps next day, I went for a long
walk with Vladimir Ilyich. He showed me Westminster (from
outside) and some other architectural landmarks. I do not
remember how he actually said it, but the inflection in his
voice meant: That's *their* famous Westminister. "Their"
meant, of course, not the one belonging to the English, but
belonging to the enemy. This inflection in Lenin's voice, seemingly accidental, was organically his own; it was this tone of
voice which always made its appearance when Lenin spoke
about some cultural treasures or new achievements, about the
arrangements of the British Museum, about the wealth of information contained in *The Times,* and also, many years later,
about German artillery or French air force. *They know, they
have got, they made it, they achieved*—yes, but what foes they
are! In his eyes the shadow of the exploiting classes lay over
the whole human culture, and this shadow was always as visible to him as daylight.

As far as I can remember, I showed a very slight interest in
the architecture of London. Suddenly transported from Verkholensk, straight out of Russia—I found myself abroad for
the first time—I was taking in Vienna, Paris, and London in
a rather summary manner and could hardly notice such "de-

---

[1] *Translator's note:* Point of illegal crossing of the frontier.
[2] *Translator's note:* Member of the Social Revolutionary Party.

tails" as Westminster Abbey. Besides, Vladimir Ilyich had
something else in mind when he took me for the long walk.
He wanted to get to know me and to test me. And indeed "the
whole *curriculum*" became the subject of the test. Answering
his questions, I described the composition of the colony of deportees on the Lena and the inner groupings which were forming themselves. The main line of division between various
tendencies was marked by the attitude toward active political
struggle, toward the principle of centralism in the organization, and toward terrorism.

"Well, and were there no theoretical differences of opinion
in connection with Bernstein's views?" asked V. I. I told him
how we read Bernstein's book and Kautsky's reply to it in the
Moscow prison and later on in exile. In our group none of the
Marxists sided with Bernstein. It was taken for granted that
Kautsky's view was the correct one. But we did not see any
connection between the theoretical struggle then proceeding
on an international scale and our organizational-political
quarrels; we did not even give a thought to the idea that there
might be a connection between the two, at least not until the
first copies of *Iskra* and Lenin's book *What Is to Be Done?*
appeared in the Lena colonies. I was relating to him that we
had read with great interest the first philosophical works of
Bogdanov.[3] I remember very clearly Vladimir Ilyich's remark.
He also thought that the little book on nature written from
the materialistic point of view was very valuable, but Plekhanov did not approve of it, saying that this was not materialism.
V. I. had as yet no definite opinion about the subject; he only
related the view of Plekhanov with great respect for his authority on philosophical matters, but also with some perplexity. I too was amazed at Plekhanov's assessment of the book.

Then V. I. asked some question on economics. I told him

---

[3] *Translator's note:* Bogdanov (Malinovsky), Alexander Alexandrovich
(1873–1928), philosopher and economist, from 1896 a Social Democrat, in
1903 joined the Bolsheviks.

how in the Moscow transfer prison we collectively studied his volume on *The Development of Capitalism in Russia,* and how in exile we worked over *Das Kapital,* stopping, however, at the second volume. I remarked on the tremendous amount of statistical data presented in *The Development of Capitalism.* In the Moscow prison we commented many a time on this massive work.

"Yes, but this was not done all at once," answered Lenin.

Obviously it gave him pleasure to learn that young comrades paid great attention to his most important book on economics.

Then we talked about Makhaisky and about the impression his theory made on the exiles, and about those who succumbed to it. I related that the first hectographed pamphlet by Makhaisky to reach us on the Lena came from "high up" and made quite an impact on the majority of people because of its violent critique of Social Democratic opportunism; in this sense it agreed with our way of thinking provoked by the Kautsky-Bernstein polemic. The second pamphlet in which Makhaisky "tears down the mask" of Marx's formulation of production laws, seeing in it a theoretical justification for the exploitation of the proletariat by the intelligentsia, aroused our indignation and caused confusion. Finally, we received later the third pamphlet, containing a positive program in which the remnants of "economism" were mixed up with the germs of syndicalism—this seemed to us completely incoherent.

We talked about my future work only in most general terms, on that occasion. First of all, I wanted to acquaint myself with what had been published recently, and then I intended to return illegally to Russia. It was decided that I should, for the time being, "look around" a little.

I had to find some lodgings, and Nadezhda Konstantinovna took me to a different district of London, to the house where Vera Zasulich, Martov, and also Blumenfeld lived. Blumenfeld was in charge of the *Iskra* printing shop. There was a room vacant there which I took. The house was typically English. The living space was organized not horizontally but vertically, with the owner living on the lowest floor, and then one over another the lodgers. There was also one common room which Plekhanov, on his very first visit, nicknamed "the den." Primarily because of Vera Zasulich, but not without the active cooperation of Martov, this room was always in a state of terrible disorder. Here we drank coffee, met for discussions, smoked, etc.

This was how the short period of my London existence began. I threw myself with avidity on the copies of *Iskra* and the pamphlets of *Zaria*. This too was the time when I began to work for *Iskra*. I think that my first contribution to *Iskra* consisted of a note on the occasion of the twentieth anniversary of the Schlüsselburg fortress. The note ended with a quotation from Homer, or rather from Homer's Russian translator Gnedich, about the "invincible hands" with which the revolution would take czarism in its grip (on the way from Siberia I had read the *Iliad* very thoroughly). Lenin liked the note. But he had some legitimate doubts about those "invincible hands" and expressed them to me with a benevolent smile. "But this is a quotation from Homer," I replied to justify myself, yet I readily agreed that the classical quotation was not indispensable. My note can be found in the *Iskra,* but without the "invincible hands."

It was also then that I gave my first lectures in Whitechapel, where I had to join battle with the "old" Tchaikovsky (he was already an old man at that time) and with the anarchist Tcherkezov, who was not a young man either. I was sincerely astonished that such famous gray-bearded emigrés were capable of talking such complete nonsense . . . The Marxist emigré Alexeev, who was an "old Londoner" in close contact with the *Iskra* people, became my link with Whitechapel. It was he who introduced me to the "English way of life" and, generally speaking, became the "fount of all knowledge" in this field.

I remember a particular conversation I had with him on our way to Whitechapel and back. I repeated to Vladimir Ilyich the two views which Alexeev expressed, one on the manner in which the change in the Russian political regime would occur, and the other on the last book by Kautsky. In Russia, said Alexeev, the change will not come about gradually, but rather violently, precisely as a result of the *rigidity*[4] of autocracy. The word "rigidity" (rudeness, hardness, inflexibility) engraved itself on my memory. "Well," said Lenin, "he may be right, after all." The second was Alexeev's opinion about Kautsky's work under the title *On the Morrow of the Social Revolution*. I knew that Lenin was very interested in the book and that, as he said himself, he had read it twice and was reading it for the third time; it seemed to me that he even revised the Russian translation. As for myself, I had just finished diligently perusing it on the recommendation of Vladimir Ilyich. Alexeev, incidentally, maintained that Kautsky's work was "opportunistic."

"Id-iot," Lenin said unexpectedly, pouting his lips angrily —always a sign of his displeasure.

Alexeev's attitude toward Lenin was very respectful. "I think he is more important for the revolution than Plekhanov." I did not, of course, mention this to Lenin, but I repeated Alexeev's words to Martov who did not react.

The editorial board of *Iskra* and *Zaria* consisted of six people: three "old" members—Plekhanov, Zasulich, and Axelrod —and three young ones—Lenin, Martov, and Potresov. Plekhanov and Axelrod lived in Switzerland and Vera Zasulich in London with the younger members. Potresov was at that time somewhere on the continent. This dispersal caused technical difficulties, which, however, did not worry Lenin; on the contrary, he seemed to be quite pleased. Before my departure

[4] *Translator's note:* In English in the original.

for the continent, Lenin initiated me delicately into the internal affairs of the editorial board; he also told me that Plekhanov insisted that all the editors should move to Switzerland, but that he, Lenin, was against the transfer because this would only make work more difficult. This remark made me vaguely aware for the first time, that the editorial board remained in London not only as the result of some police regulations but also because of personal and organizational reasons. In day-to-day political work Lenin sought the maximum independence from the "old" members and first of all from Plekhanov, with whom he was already in serious conflict especially over the elaboration of the party program.

The mediators in such cases were Vera Zasulich and Martov. In this duel Zasulich played the role of Plekhanov's second, while Martov that of Lenin's. Both mediators were of a conciliatory disposition and also very friendly toward each other. Only gradually did I learn about the sharp clashes which occurred between Plekhanov and Lenin when they tried to work out the theoretical parts of the program of the party. I remember that Vladimir Ilyich asked my opinion of this program, which had just been published (in *Iskra,* November 25, if I am not mistaken). I had, however, read the program in its broad outlines, so that I was unable to answer the more specific questions which were of interest to Lenin. The disagreements concerned the necessity—in Lenin's view—of defining more decisively and categorically the character of capitalism and its tendencies; the concentration of production; the decline of the intermediate strata; class differentiation, etc. . . . Plekhanov treated these subjects with some reserve and not at all sharply. The program was sprinkled with expressions like "more or less" which came directly from Plekhanov's pen.

As far as I remember, Martov and Zasulich told me that the first draft which Lenin wrote as a counter to Plekhanov's met with the harsh judgment and haughty sneers, so characteristic of Plekhanov in such circumstances. Of course, this was not the way either to discourage Lenin or to intimidate him. Their struggle took on quite a dramatic turn. Vera Ivanovna (Zasulich) herself repeated what she used to say to Lenin: "Georgi (Plekhanov) is like a greyhound: he will shake you and shake you and will let you go; you are like a bulldog: you have a deadly grip." I remember this and also Vera's final remark: "Lenin was very pleased. 'So I have a deadly grip, have I?' he asked delightedly." Vera imitated Lenin's intonation with much amusement in telling the story.

During my stay in London Plekhanov came over for a short trip. I saw him then for the first time. He came to our common lodgings and to our "den," but I was not at home.

"George has arrived," announced Vera Ivanovna, "he wants to see you; go to his room."

"Which George?" I asked, intrigued, thinking that there must be some famous personality still unknown to me.

"Well, Plekhanov . . . We call him George."

I went to see him in the evening. In a small room I found him with the well-known German Social Democratic writer Beer and an Englishman, Askew. All the chairs were occupied, and Plekhanov, not without hesitation, proposed that I should sit on the bed. I took this as a matter of course, without realizing that for Plekhanov, every inch a European, such unconventionalities of behavior were permissible only in extreme circumstances. The talk was in German in which Plekhanov was not fluent; he answered in monosyllables only. Beer talked first about the clever way in which the English bourgeoisie was winning over the most outstanding workers; then the discussion touched on the English forerunners of French materialism. Beer and Askew left soon afterward. Georgi Valentinovich expected, not unreasonably, that I would leave with them. It was already late and one was anxious not to disturb the neighbors. For me, however, the real conversation was now about to begin.

"What Beer said was quite interesting," I opened.

"Yes, what he said about English politics was interesting, but what he said about philosophy was trash," answered Plekhanov.

As I was not making a move to leave, Georgi Valentinovich proposed that we should go out for a glass of beer. He asked me a few unimportant questions, was amiable, but in his amiability there was a trace of concealed impatience. I felt that his attention was on other things. It was possible that he was simply tired after the journey. But I parted from him with a feeling of dissatisfaction and irritation.

During the London period, as well as later in Geneva, I used to meet with Zasulich and Martov much more often than Lenin. In London living in the same house, and in Geneva eating in the same small restaurants, Zasulich, Martov, and I used to see each other several times a day, while with Lenin, who led more of a family life, every meeting, apart from official gatherings, became something of a minor event.

Vera Zasulich was an exceptional person; she was also charming in a peculiar manner. She wrote very slowly, truly suffering all the torments of creation. "Vera does not write," Vladimir Ilyich said once, "she composes a mosaic." She did, indeed, put down on paper one sentence at a time, pacing up and down her room, shuffling in her slippers, chain-smoking cigarettes which she rolled by herself, throwing butts in all corners of the room, on the windowsills, on the table, scattering ash over her blouse, her arms, her manuscript, her tea, and incidentally also over her interlocutor. She was, and she remained to the end, the old type of radical intellectual with Marxism grafted on to her by fate. Her articles proved that she had assimilated remarkably well the theoretical elements of Marxism; but at the same time there persisted in her untouched the moral-political foundations of a Russian radical of the 1870's. In more intimate talks she allowed herself to question some assumptions or conclusions of Marxism. The word "revolutionary" had for her a particular meaning devoid of any connotation of class consciousness. I remember the talk we had about her "Revolutionaries among the Bourgeoisie." I used the expression "bourgeois-democratic revolutionaries." "Well, no," interjected Vera with annoyance, or rather with sorrow, "no, neither bourgeois nor proletarian but simply revolutionaries. One can, of course, say '*petit bourgeois* revolutionaries,' " she added, "if one includes into *petit bourgeois* all that one cannot place anywhere else . . ."

At that time the ideological center of Social Democracy was Germany, and we were tensely watching the struggle between the orthodox Social Democrats and the revisionists. But Vera Ivanovna, who thought little of all this, would say suddenly: "Well, well. They will finish with revisionism, they will reestablish Marx, they will get a majority, and in spite of it all they will live with their Kaiser."

"Which 'they,' Vera Ivanovna?"

"Well, the German Social Democrats, of course."

On this point, incidentally, her judgment proved more correct than it seemed at the time, although things happened in a different way and for different reasons than she expected . . .

She skeptically viewed the plan of the distribution of land —not that she rejected it, but she treated it with a great deal of good humor.

I remember the following episode. Shortly before the Congress, Konstantin Konstantinovich Bauer came to Geneva. He was one of the old Marxists, a rather unbalanced man, who at one time had been a friend of Struve, but who now hesitated between *Iskra* and the *Osvobozhdenia*.[5] In Geneva he became more attracted to *Iskra,* but refused to accept the

---

[5] *Translator's note: Osvobozhdenia,* translated "Liberation," was the organ of a group which soon founded the Constitutional Democratic Party (Kadets). Its emphasis was on liberty and democracy, whereas *Iskra,* "The Spark," gave birth to the Social Democratic Party, and its emphasis was on "the spark that shall become the flame," namely on social revolution.

principle of *otrezki*.[6] He went to see Lenin, whom he probably knew. He returned unconverted, however, most likely because Lenin, knowing his Hamlet-like doubts, did not bother to convert him. I knew Bauer from the time of deportation, and now I had a very long discussion with him about this unfortunate problem. With the sweat of my brow I set forth all the arguments which I had managed to assemble during the six months of endless debate with the Social Revolutionaries and all the other opponents of the agrarian program of *Iskra*. And then, that very evening Martov (I think it was Martov) announced at the meeting of the editorial board, in my presence, that Bauer came to him and declared himself finally to be an *Iskra*-man. "Well, well, Trotsky scattered to the winds all his doubts . . ."

"And about the distribution as well?" Vera Zasulich inquired anxiously.

"Especially about the *otrezki*."

"Poor chap!" she exclaimed with such a comic intonation that we all burst out laughing.

"With Vera Ivanovna much is built on moral foundations, on sentiments," Lenin said one day. Both she and Martov, Lenin went on, were sometimes tempted to defend terroristic methods, for example, when Val, the Governor of Vilna, ordered workers who took part in a demonstration to be flogged. Traces of this particular "deviation," as we would call it now, can be found in one of the copies of *Iskra*. This is how, I think, it had happened: Martov and Zasulich were editing a copy of the paper while Lenin was on the continent. Tele-

[6] *Translator's note: Otrezki* refers to Lenin's attempt to give the peasants some "immediate demand" which would mobilize them against the authorities just as demands for higher wages and shorter hours were to mobilize the working man. The Emancipation of 1861 freed the peasants from bondage and granted to them possession of most of the land that they had personally been tilling. Lenin here is not urging the Socialist Revolutionary demand, "distribution of all the land," but was merely asking for the restitution of these small bits of land, *otrezki,* to the peasants.

graphic agencies brought a report about the flogging in Vilna. This awakened in Vera Ivanovna the old heroic radical who shot Trepov because he ordered the birching of political prisoners. Martov supported her . . . Lenin, when he received the fresh copy of *Iskra,* was indignant. "This is the first step on the road to capitulation before the Social Revolutionaries and their doctrine!"

At the same time Plekhanov sent his protest. This incident had taken place before my arrival in London so that in what I am relating here there might be some factual inaccuracies. But I remember very well the heart of the affair.

"Of course, it is not a matter of adopting terrorism as a method," Vera Zasulich tried to explain, "but it seems to me that perhaps terrorism may teach them not to flog people . . ."

Vera could not really conduct a serious debate—nor could she speak in public. She never answered her opponent's argument directly; she muttered something to herself and then, all aflame, spurted out a profusion of sentences, so fast that she was nearly choking; and she addressed herself not to the person who had questioned her, but to someone who, she hoped, would be able to understand her.

If discussion was more formal, with a chairman, Vera Zasulich never asked for the inclusion of her name on the list of speakers; in order to say something she had to be in a state of fever. But in that state she would hold forth without paying any attention to the formal procedure, which she treated with utter contempt. She always interrupted the speaker and the chairman and would go on talking until she had said what was on her mind. In order to understand her, one had to follow her trend of thought closely; her ideas—whether she was right or wrong—were always interesting and always peculiarly her own. One can imagine what a contrast there was between Vera Ivanovna, with her diffuse radicalism, her subjectivity, and her turbulence, and Vladimir Ilyich. It was not that they disliked each other, but there was a feeling of deep organic incompatibility. Her psychological insight made her realize Lenin's strength, which she viewed with vague hostility; this showed itself in her expression about Lenin's "deadly grip."

Only gradually, and not without difficulty, was I becoming aware of the complexity of relationships between the members of the editorial board. As I said before, I came to London like a raw provincial in more senses than one. Not only had I never been abroad, I had never even seen Petersburg! In Moscow, just as in Kiev, I had only been in the transfer prison. I knew the Marxist authors only from their writings. In Siberia I had read a few copies of *Iskra* and also Lenin's *What Is to Be Done?* I had heard of the author of *The Development of Capitalism* in the Moscow prison (from Vanovsky, I think) only as a rising star of Social Democracy. About Martov I knew little, about Potresov—nothing. In London, reading with avidity *Iskra, Zaria,* and all our other publications, I came across, in *Zaria,* a brilliant article, on the role and significance of trade unions, directed against Prokopovich. "Who is this Molotov?" I asked Martov. "That is Parvus"; I knew nothing about Parvus either. I accepted *Iskra* as an entity, and during these months it did not occur to me (I even had an inner reluctance) to look for differences of views, tendencies, for opposing influences either in the paper or among the editors.

I noticed that some leading articles and *feuilletons* in *Iskra,* although not signed, were written in the first person: "In such-and-such an issue I said" or "as I already wrote" and so on. I inquired who was the author of these pieces. It turned out that it was Lenin. I remarked that there was some literary awkwardness in using first person singular in an unsigned article.

"Why do you think so?" asked Lenin, intrigued, believing perhaps that my remark was not quite casual, or that I expressed more than a personal opinion.

"I don't know, but it seems so to me," I answered vaguely because I had nothing more precise to say on this matter.

"I do not think so." Lenin chuckled enigmatically.

At that time one might have perceived a trace of "egocentrism" in this literary form. However, by giving to his articles, even the unsigned ones, a specific style, Lenin took full personal responsibility for their political line—evidently he was not quite sure that this line was shared by his close collaborators. Here we had, on a small scale, the persistence, the stubbornness of Lenin. *His whole being was geared to one great purpose,* and he would make use of any circumstance and disregard all formalities in straining toward his goal—this was indeed Lenin the leader.

Iskra was under Lenin's political direction; the main contributor was, however, Martov. He wrote with ease, and interminably; and he gave talks as well. Lenin used to spend a great deal of time in the British Museum on theoretical studies. One day he was found in the library writing a polemical article against Nadezhdin, who at that time stood politically somewhere between the Social Democrats and the Social Revolutionaries and had his own little publication in Switzerland. The night before, Martov (who usually worked at night) managed to write his own long contribution about Nadezhdin.

"Have you read Julius' article on Nadezhdin?" Lenin asked when I met him at the Museum.

"Yes," I answered.

"What do you think of it?"

"It seems good."

"Well," said Lenin, "maybe it is good, but it is not precise enough. He does not draw the conclusions. I have drafted something here"—and he handed me a small sheet of paper covered with his handwriting in pencil—"and now I do not know what to do. Should I add this as supplementary remarks to Julius' article?"

The next issue of *Iskra* carried Martov's article with notes

by Lenin at the bottom of the page. Both the article and the
notes were unsigned. I do not know whether these notes are
included in Lenin's collected *Works,* but I can vouch for their
authorship.

A few months later and some weeks before the Congress a
sharp disagreement flared up between Lenin and Martov on
the attitude to be taken toward street demonstrations, or, to
be more precise, on armed struggle with the police. Lenin
maintained that it was necessary to form small armed groups
so that militant workers should learn how to fight the police.
Martov disagreed. The dispute came before the editors.
"Would not this give rise to something like group terrorism?"
was my comment on Lenin's point of view. (One should remember that at that time we were very much against the terroristic tactics of the Social Revolutionaries.) Martov took up
the question and started developing the idea that one should
teach the demonstrators to defend themselves against attacks
by the police, but not to organize groups which would fight
them. Plekhanov, toward whom I and probably also others
looked expectantly, refrained from speaking; he proposed that
Martov should write a draft resolution so that we could discuss the controversial issue, text in hand. However, the whole
question was lost in the mass of other events and problems
connected with the Congress.

I had very few occasions to observe Lenin and Martov in
private, beyond our conferences and meetings. Lenin disliked
those long palavers, formless debates, and interminable cha-
otic conversations which inevitably led to emigré gossip and
empty chatter. Martov, however, was inclined to this kind of
pastime. Lenin, this most powerful "engineer of revolution,"
had only one goal before his eyes, and toward this final goal
he was pressing, whether in politics or in his theoretical or
philosophical studies, in discussions with others or in learning
foreign languages. His was perhaps the most determined utilitarianism ever produced in the laboratory of history. But as

this utilitarianism was harnessed to a grand design, it did not diminish or impoverish Lenin's personality—on the contrary, with the growth of experience and with the ever-widening scale of action, his personality was constantly developing and expanding.

Side by side with Lenin, Martov, his closest companion in arms, was already beginning to feel ill at ease. They still addressed each other in the familiar second person singular, but a certain coolness was creeping into their relations. Martov lived much more in the present with day-to-day vexations, day-to-day literary and journalistic writings, day-to-day news, polemics, and conversations. Lenin, although firmly entrenched in the present, was always trying to pierce the veil of the future. Martov evolved innumerable and often brilliant guesses, hypotheses, and propositions, which he himself promptly forgot; whereas Lenin waited and developed his when he needed them. The elaborate subtlety of Martov's ideas made Lenin anxiously shake his head. At that time the difference in their political thinking was not yet defined—indeed, it was hardly perceptible; only in retrospect does it seem visible now. Later on, during the split at the Second Congress, the collaborators of *Iskra* became divided into the *hard* and the *soft*. This terminology was very much used at that time, precisely because the lines of division were not yet rigid; there were rather differences in approach to certain problems than in the degree of determination to go on to the very end.

As to the differences between Lenin and Martov, one can say that even before the split, before the Congress, Lenin was *hard* and Martov *soft*. And they both knew it. Lenin would glance at Martov, whom he highly esteemed, with a critical and somewhat suspicious look; and Martov, feeling this glance, grew uneasy and his thin shoulders would twitch nervously. When they met and talked afterward, at least in my presence, one missed the friendly inflection of the voice and the jests. Lenin would look beyond Martov as he talked, while

Martov's eyes would grow glassy under his spectacles, drooping and never cleaned. And when Lenin spoke with me about Martov, his voice had a peculiar tone. "Oh, I see. Julius said so?"—and the name Julius was pronounced in a special way, with a slight emphasis, as if to give a warning—"Yes, yes, a good man, even a remarkable one, but very, very soft."

Undoubtedly Vera Ivanovna also had a certain influence on Martov—not a political but a psychological one; and she kept him at a distance from Lenin. Of course, all I am saying here is more of a psychological characterization than a statement of facts, and it concerns the situation as I saw it more than twenty-two years ago. During these years many events impressed themselves on my memory, and I may be committing an error here and there in relating these vague sentiments on personal relationships. How much do we remember and what part does our imagination—unintentionally—play in reconstructing the past? I think that in essentials I do remember what had happened and how it had happened.

After my, so to say, trial appearances in Whitechapel (Alexeev used to give a "report" to the members of the editorial board), I was sent on a lecture tour to Brussels, to Liège, and to Paris. My subject was: "What is historical materialism and how do the Revolutionary Socialists understand it?" Vladimir Ilyich found this subject of great interest, and he looked through my plan of the lecture, my notes and quotations. He suggested that I should work it over and prepare it for publication in *Zaria*; but I never had the courage to do this.

From Paris I was recalled by telegram to London. There was talk of sending me into Russia illegally. Vladimir Ilyich thought this would be useful. Comrades in Russia complained of bad organization, of lack of personnel, and I think that Clair-Kzhizhanovsky also asked for my return. But even before I reached London, the plan was changed. L. G. Deutsch, who then lived in London and was always very friendly toward me, told me later on how he intervened "in my favor," maintaining that "the youngster" (he never called me anything else) should be allowed to stay abroad in order to study; after some opposition, Lenin agreed with him. To work in the Russian organization of *Iskra* was a very tempting proposal; however, I was quite pleased to remain abroad for some time.

One Sunday I went with Vladimir Ilyich and Nadezhda Konstantinovna to a socialist church: a Social Democratic gathering there was accompanied by singing of pious revolutionary hymns. The main speaker was a composer who returned from Australia, if I am not mistaken. Vladimir Ilyich in a whisper was translating his speech for our benefit; at that time, at least, it sounded quite revolutionary. Then everybody stood up and sang: "Almighty God, put an end to all kings and all rich men . . ." or something to that effect. "The English proletariat has in itself many revolutionary and socialist elements," said Lenin when we left the church, "but they are all mixed up with conservatism, with religion and prejudices; and there seems to be no way in which these elements can come to the top." It may be of interest to note that Vera Zasulich and Martov lived without any contact with the English working class movement whatsoever: *Iskra* and all that happened around it absorbed them completely. Lenin, at least from time to time, made some independent reconnoitering into the state of that movement.

There is no need to say that Vladimir Ilyich, Nadezhda Konstantinovna, and her mother lived extremely simply. On our return from the Social Democratic church we had lunch in the small kitchen in their two-room flat. I remember, as if it were yesterday, the thin slices of meat served straight from the frying pan. Then we took tea. As usual, they were poking fun at me, asking whether I would be able to find my way home; being methodical, I classified my inefficiency as "topographical cretinism." The streets were still unfamiliar to me.

The date of the Congress was approaching, and finally the

decision was taken to transfer the *Iskra* center to Geneva. Life there was incomparably cheaper; it was also easier to maintain contact from there with Russia. Very reluctantly Lenin agreed. I went first to Paris and, from there, together with Martov arrived in Geneva. The work preparatory to the Congress became more intense. Soon Lenin also came to Paris. He was to give three lectures on the agrarian problems at the so-called High School which was set up in Paris by university professors exiled from Russia. A group of Marxist students insisted on inviting Lenin after a lecture had been given by Chernov. The professors were not a little worried and asked the militant lecturer not to indulge in any polemics. Lenin, however, did not feel bound by any conditions and began his first lecture by stating that Marxism, being a revolutionary theory, was *ipso facto* highly controversial, but that this in no way detracted from its scientific character.

Before the first lecture, I remember, Vladimir Ilyich was very nervous. But once on the rostrum he became quite composed, at least outwardly. Professor Gambarov, who came to listen, summed up his impressions to Deutsch: "A real professor!" The kind man meant in this way to pay the highest tribute to Lenin. The lectures were full of polemics against the Narodniks and against the agrarian social reformism of David, whom Lenin compared and put on the same level; and yet throughout the speaker remained within the bounds of economic theory, mentioning neither the current political struggle nor the agrarian program of the Social Democrats nor that of the Social Revolutionaries.

These were the limits which Lenin imposed on himself in view of the academic character of his audience. But after the third lecture he made a political speech on the subject of agrarian reform not at the High School but at 110 Rue Choisy (if I remember correctly), at a meeting organized by the French group of *Iskra*. The hall was crowded. All the students from the High School came to hear the practical conclusions drawn from the theoretical exposition to which they had been treated at the school. Under discussion was the agrarian program of *Iskra* and, in particular, the problem of the restitution of the *otrezki*. I do not remember who spoke as Lenin's opponent; but I do remember that Lenin was excellent in his conclusions. One of the French *Iskra*-men said to me when we were leaving the hall, "Lenin surpassed himself tonight!" After the meeting the organizers, by custom, took the lecturer to a café. All were delighted and the lecturer himself pleasantly excited. The treasurer, very gratified, announced the receipts from the sale of entrance tickets. *Iskra* made something like 75 or 100 francs from the lecture—a sum not to be despised. All this was at the beginning of 1903. I cannot give a more precise date, but this should not be too difficult to establish— it may have been established already.

During this visit to Paris it was decided that Lenin should see an opera. N. I. Sedova, a member of the *Iskra* group, was to organize the evening. Lenin carried with him the briefcase which he took to the High School. The performance consisted of *Louise* by Massenet (?),[7] an opera with a more or less democratic theme. We all sat together in the gallery. Apart from Lenin, Sedova, and myself, there was also Martov and others whose names I do not remember. There is a little incident connected with this visit to the Opéra Comique which has nothing in common with music. Lenin had bought, in Paris, a pair of shoes which proved to be too tight. He suffered for a few hours and finally decided to get rid of them. It so happened that my own shoes were in a very poor state and Lenin gave me his new pair which at the beginning seemed to fit me quite well, and I decided to wear them on the outing to the opera. On the way there everything went smoothly. But during the opera I began to feel very uncomfortable. This was probably the reason why I do not remember either my own or Lenin's impressions of the performance; but I do remem-

[7] *Translator's note: Louise* was actually by Gustave Charpentier.

ber that Lenin was in a good mood, jesting and laughing. On our way back my suffering became intolerable, with Vladimir Ilyich cruelly amusing himself at my expense. There was, however, some compassion underneath his laughter. Hadn't he also had a few hours of discomfort in the very same shoes?

I have mentioned Lenin's nervousness before his lectures in Paris; I feel I must return to this remark. Lenin experienced this kind of nervousness before public appearances even later, and the less congenial the audience, the more formal the occasion, the greater would be his agitation. As a speaker Lenin always seemed full of self-confidence; he spoke with energy and so fast that the stenographers had a hard job keeping up with him. But when he was ill at ease, his voice seemed not his own and sounded like an echo—impersonal and coming from afar. However, when he felt that *this* particular audience was really in need of learning just what *he* had to say, his voice acquired all its vivacity, flexibility, and persuasiveness, not of the "oratorical" kind, but the conversational one, adapted to the needs of the rostrum. There was no art of oratory in Lenin's speeches, yet his was more than uncommon eloquence. One may, of course, say that every speaker addresses the audience he feels to be "his" with more ease and success; this is perfectly true. The question arises, however, what circumstances and what audience make the speaker feel himself among "his" listeners. European orators of the type of a Vanderwelde, brought up in the Parliamentary tradition, need a certain degree of solemnity and a formal atmosphere in order to achieve an effect. They feel most relaxed at formal or official celebrations. For Lenin any such gathering was a minor disaster. His most brilliant and convincing speeches were those in which he analyzed the problems of political struggle. He was probably at his best when addressing the members of the Central Committee on the eve of October.

Before his lectures in Paris, I think I heard Lenin speak only once before in London, about the end of December, 1902.

It is strange that I have no recollection either of the occasion or of the subject matter of the speech. I even seem to doubt whether it really was Lenin who spoke then. But surely a large meeting of Russians in London was an important event; Lenin would not have been there if he was not going to address it. The only way I can explain this lapse of memory is the following: In all probability Lenin devoted his lecture to the same subject which was discussed in the leading article of the current copy of *Iskra*. By that time I had already had the opportunity to read Lenin's article, so that his speech held nothing new for me; after the lecture there was no debate: Among the "Londoners" there were no opponents confident enough to contradict Lenin. Part of the audience consisted of anarchists and part of the members of the *Bund*; as the atmosphere was not very gratifying, the whole occasion vanished without leaving any impression. I only remember that at the end of the meeting I was approached by the couple B. who had belonged to the former Petersburg group of *Rabochaya Mysl* (*Workers' Thought*) and had lived for quite a time in London. "Come to us on New Year's eve," they said. (This is why I remember that the meeting took place at the end of December.) "What for?" I asked, like a real barbarian. "Well, we shall spend the evening in a circle of comrades. Ulyanov will come, and Krupskaya will be there." I remember that they said "Ulyanov" and not Lenin, so that at first I did not realize whom they were talking about. It turned out that Vera Zasulich and Martov were also invited. Next day in "the den" we deliberated what to do; then we inquired whether Lenin was going. In the end, I think, nobody went. This was a pity. It would have been a unique opportunity to see Lenin with Zasulich and Martov in the atmosphere of a New Year's party.

After my arrival from Paris in Geneva I was invited, together with Zasulich and Martov, to see Plekhanov; I think Vladimir Ilyich came too. I have a very blurred recollection of that evening. In any case, it was not a political gathering, but a "social," not to say a philistine one. I remember that I sat there rather helpless and bored; from time to time the host or the hostess gave me some attention—otherwise I did not know what to do with myself. Plekhanov's daughters were serving tea and cakes; there was some tension in the air and probably I was not the only one to feel ill at ease. Or perhaps I felt the coolness much more sharply because I was so much younger? This was my first and last visit there and, of course, my impressions were fleeting and perhaps casual, as casual and as fleeting as were all my encounters with Plekhanov. I have tried to give a short character study of that brilliant Marxist teacher and the foremost master of Marxism in Russia, in other writings; here I want to convey only my impressions of my first contact in which—alas—I was not very fortunate. Zasulich, worried by this unhappy state of affairs, used to say, "I know that George can be impossible, but, really, he is quite a nice animal." (This was her favorite eulogy.)

I should like to mention here that in the home of the Axelrods the atmosphere was one of simplicity and sincere comradeship. To this day I remember with gratitude the hours I spent at the Axelrods' hospitable family table during my frequent trips to Zurich. Vladimir Ilyich spent much time there too, and to judge from the way the Axelrods spoke about his visits, he must have appreciated their warmth and cordiality. It so happened that I never met Lenin in Axelrod's home.

Vera Zasulich's attitude toward young comrades, her simplicity and friendliness, were quite exceptional. If one could not speak about her "hospitality," it is only because she was more in need of it herself than she ever could offer. She lived, ate, and dressed like the most modest of students. Her only passions, in a material sense, were tobacco and mustard, and she consumed both in huge quantities. When she covered the thinnest slice of ham with a thick layer of mustard, we used to say, "Vera Ivanovna is feasting!"

L. G. Deutsch, the fourth member of the group of *Emanci-*

pation of Labor, was also remarkably kind and attentive toward the young. I have failed to mention that, as the manager of *Iskra,* Deutsch took part in the editorial meetings in which he had a consultative voice. He usually followed Plekhanov, and his views in the matter of revolutionary tactics were more than moderate. One day, to my utter amazement, he declared, "There won't be any armed uprising, young man, and there is no need for it. In deportation we also had those pugnacious cocks who at the slightest provocation went into battle and were destroyed. My attitude was different: to stand firm, to make the administration understand that it might come to a big battle, but never get involved. In this way I gained both the respect of the administration and the softening of the regime. We should adopt the same tactics toward czarism, otherwise we shall be beaten and destroyed without any advantage to the cause."

This tactical prognostication was so stupefying that I repeated it to Martov and to Zasulich and to Lenin. I forgot Martov's reaction, but Vera Ivanovna said, " 'Eugene' "—this was Deutsch's old pseudonym—"was always like that. Personally a man of exceptional courage, but politically extremely prudent and moderate." Lenin listened to me, then muttered something like "Hm . . . Hm . . . Yea," and we both burst out laughing without expressing any opinion.

The delegates to the Second Congress began arriving in Geneva, and we began an unending series of meetings. In this preparatory work Lenin indisputably—though not always obviously—played the leading role. There were meetings of the *Iskra* editorial board, and meetings of the *Iskra* organization; separate meetings with groups of delegates and separate plenary sessions; some delegates were full of doubts or reservations, or brought with them complaints or grievances. These preliminaries absorbed a great deal of time.

Only three workers came to take part in the Congress. Lenin entered into long discussions with each of them, and won them over. One was Shotman from Petersburg, a very young but sensible and thoughtful man. After one such talk with Lenin he came back—we stayed in the same lodgings—and kept on repeating, "And how his small eyes were sparkling—one would think he can see through . . ."

The delegate from Nikolaev was Kalafati. Vladimir Ilyich questioned me about him in great detail, as I knew him still at Nikolaev, and then, smiling slyly, remarked, "He said he knew you when you were something of a Tolstoyan?"

"Oh, what nonsense," I answered, almost indignant.

"Well, what's wrong with that?" said Lenin, half-teasing and half-reassuring. "You were then about eighteen years old, and, you know, people are not born Marxists."

"Yes, that's true, but I certainly had nothing in common with Tolstoyanism."

In the preliminary discussions a great deal of attention was given to the formulation of the statutes; and the most important problem was that of the structure of the organization, which was to determine the relations between its central journal and its central committee. I had come abroad with the idea that the "central organ," that is the journal, should be "subordinated" to the Central Committee. The majority of the *Iskra*-men in Russia held this view, though neither very clearly nor in a very determined manner.

"This will not work," insisted Lenin, "because of the relation of forces . . . Well, how will they direct us from inside Russia? No, it won't work . . . We constitute the stable center, and we shall direct affairs from here."

One of the resolutions demanded that the "central organ" should undertake to publish articles written by members of the Central Committee.

"Even those articles which go against the 'central organ'?" asked Lenin.

"Of course."

"What for? This will not do. A controversy among two

members of the 'central organ' might in certain circumstances
be of some use, but a polemic of the Central Committee members who are in Russia against the 'central organ' outside Russia is unacceptable."

"In that case the 'central organ' will exercise a complete
dictatorship?" I asked.

"What's wrong with that?" retorted Lenin. "In our present
situation it cannot be otherwise."

A great deal of confusion was caused by the so-called right
of co-option. At one of the meetings we, that is the young
ones, reached the decision that there should be a right of
"positive co-option" and of "negative co-option."

"But what you call 'negative co-option' means in good Russian the right to chuck someone out," laughed Vladimir Ilyich
next morning. "It is not so simple. Well, you just try to apply
—ha! ha! ha!—your 'right of negative co-option' to the editorial board of *Iskra!*"

For Lenin the most important problem consisted in this:
how to organize the "central organ" (that is, *Iskra*) in such a
way that in practice it should play the role of the Central
Committee as well. In his view it was impossible to preserve
the old team of "the six." On all controversial questions Zasulich and Axelrod almost invariably sided with Plekhanov,
so at best there resulted a stalemate of three votes against
three; and neither of them would ever agree to the exclusion
of anybody from the board. The only way out which remained
was its enlargement. Lenin intended to include me in the editorial team and then within it to create a smaller body of three
editors: Plekhanov, Martov, and himself. Vladimir Ilyich was
initiating me into his plan gradually; moreover, he did not
even mention to me that he had already proposed my candidature as the seventh member of the team and that this was
accepted by everybody except Plekhanov, who opposed the
whole plan with great determination. In his opinion, the admission of the seventh member automatically prejudiced the

chances of the *Emancipation of Labor* group: There would be four "young" members against three "old" ones.

I think that all this was the main reason of Plekhanov's obviously unfriendly attitude toward me. In addition, as ill luck would have it, there arose between us some disagreements which became only too plain to the delegates. First, if I am not mistaken, there was the project to set up a popular newspaper. Some delegates insisted on the need to create besides *Iskra,* a popular journal which would, if possible, be published in Russia. This was the particular project of the *Southern Worker* group, a project to which Lenin was decidedly opposed. His objections were many and varied, but the main one was the fear that a new grouping could form itself on the basis of "popular," simplified principles of Social Democracy before the kernel of the party proper became solid and well established. Plekhanov declared himself for the creation of a popular paper, firmly opposing Lenin's point of view and openly seeking the support of regional delegates. I was on Lenin's side.

At one of the meetings I argued—whether correctly or not it does not matter now—that what we needed was not a popular newspaper, but a series of propagandist pamphlets and booklets which would help the advanced workers to rise to the level of the articles in *Iskra*; that a popular publication would narrow the scope of *Iskra* and would blur the political physiognomy of the party, pushing it down to the level of "economism" and "Eserism." [8] Plekhanov objected. "Why should it blur the physiognomy of the party? Of course," he went on, "in a popular periodical we shall not be able to express everything; we shall raise certain demands, put forward certain slogans, but we shall not debate tactical problems there. We shall tell the worker that one must fight against capitalism, but, obviously, we shall not enter into a theoretical discussion on *how* one should fight against capitalism."

[8] *Translator's note:* SR's—members of the Social Revolutionary Party.

I seized upon this argument. "But the SR's and those who preach economism also say that one should fight against capitalism. We disagree with them precisely on the point of *how* to fight. If in a popular paper we do not answer this very question, we immediately blur the difference between ourselves and the SR's." My reasoning seemed convincing, and Plekhanov found no answer to it. This incident did not, of course, improve his attitude toward me. Soon we had another conflict—this time at the editorial meeting. It was decided that before the whole question of the staff of *Iskra* was finally settled by the Congress, I should participate in the meetings, without voting rights. Plekhanov categorically objected to this. Vera Ivanovna declared, "Yet, I shall bring him along." And indeed, she did "bring me along."

What went on behind the scenes I learned only much later; I appeared at the meeting knowing nothing and quite unconcerned. Plekhanov greeted me with studious coolness at which he was a past master. It so happened that at this particular meeting the editors had to concern themselves with the conflict which arose between Deutsch and Blumenfeld, whom I have already mentioned before. Deutsch was the manager of *Iskra*. Blumenfeld was in charge of the printing shop. Blumenfeld resented Deutsch's interference in the internal affairs of the printing shop. Plekhanov, in the name of old friendship, supported Deutsch and proposed that Blumenfeld should deal exclusively with the business of printing. I maintained that one cannot run a printing shop on that basis; apart from the process and techniques of printing there were also administrative and organizational questions and that in these Blumenfeld should be given a free hand. I remember the venom with which Plekhanov retorted. "No doubt Comrade Trotsky is right, in so far as on the basis of technique there arise various superstructures—administrative and others—this is exactly what the theory of historical materialism teaches us; however . . ." and so on, and so on. Lenin and Martov cautiously supported me and the appropriate resolution was accepted. But this was the last straw . . . In both incidents, as we have seen, Lenin took my side. But at the same time he observed anxiously how my relations with Plekhanov were deteriorating; this was finally threatening his whole plan for the reorganization of the editorial board. At one of the next meetings with the newly arrived delegates, Lenin took me aside and said, "About the popular paper, leave Martov to oppose Plekhanov. Martov will muddle up the whole affair—while you will hammer at it. It's better to let it lapse . . ." These expressions, "muddle up" and "hammer," I remember clearly.

After one editorial session which took place in Café Landolt, or perhaps after the session mentioned above, Zasulich, in a manner so characteristic of her, timidly yet insistently complained that we were attacking the liberals "too much." This was her sore point. "But look, they are trying hard," she said, looking past Lenin, though she was addressing herself to Lenin primarily. "In the last copy of *The Emancipation* Struve offers the example of Jaurès and calls upon Russian liberals not to break with socialism, otherwise they will be threatened with the pitiful fate of German liberalism—they should instead take their cue from French Radical-Socialists."

Lenin stood at the table, his imitation Panama hat on his head (the session was practically finished, and he was about to leave).

"One more reason to attack them strongly," he said, smiling gaily and as if teasing Vera Ivanovna.

"Well . . . Well . . . !" she exclaimed despairingly, "they make a step in our direction, and we have to 'attack them strongly'!"

"That's right. Struve tells his liberals: Against our socialism one should not behave in that coarse German fashion, but rather with French *finesse*. One should attract, bribe, deceive, corrupt in the manner of French radicals of the left who are flirting with Jaurèsism."

I have not, of course, related this memorable conversation word for word. But the sense of it and the atmosphere remain extremely vivid in my memory. At the moment I have not at hand any materials which would allow me to check the facts, but these should be quite easy to check. It would be easy enough to look through the copies of *The Emancipation* for the spring of 1903 and find Struve's article dealing with the attitude of liberals toward Democratic Socialism in general and toward Jaurèsism in particular. This article I remember precisely in connection with Vera Zasulich's words and with the incident described here. If, looking at the date of *The Emancipation,* one adds the time needed for the paper to reach Geneva, and for Vera Zasulich to read it—that is two, three, or four days—one can with enough exactitude arrive at the date of the altercation in Café Landolt. It was, as I recollect, a springlike day (it might have been early summer), the sun was shining brightly, and Lenin was smiling good-humoredly. I remember his quietly mocking voice, his self-confidence, and his "solid" figure—yes, he looked "solid," though he was then much thinner than in the last years of his life. Vera Ivanovna was, as usual, fidgety, turning this way and that; nobody, it seems, intervened in this conversation which, in any case, lasted no longer than the time it takes to get ready to leave. I returned home with Vera Ivanovna. She was depressed, feeling that Struve was beaten at his game. I could offer no consolation. None of us, however, at that time foresaw to what degree, how definitely, all the aces of Russian liberalism were trumped in that little dialogue at the entrance to Café Landolt.

I realize the inadequacy of all I have so far narrated. My story sounds poorer than I had imagined when I started on it. But I assembled carefully all that my memory retained, even episodes of little significance, because there is hardly anyone now who can describe this period in greater detail. Plekhanov is dead. Zasulich is dead. Martov is dead. And Lenin is dead. It is doubtful that any one of them should have left memoirs. Perhaps Vera Ivanovna? But we have heard nothing about it. Of the old editorial team only Axelrod and Potresov are left. But, apart from all other considerations, they both took a small part in the editorial work and were only rarely present at the editorial meetings. Deutsch would perhaps have something more to say, but he came abroad only shortly before my arrival, toward the end of the period I have been describing; besides, he was little involved directly in the work of the editorial board.

Invaluable information could be provided, and, let us hope, will be provided, by Nadezhda Konstantinovna. At that time she was in the center of all organizational activity. It was to her that newly arrived comrades reported first; she briefed and sent them off; she established contacts and clandestine connections; she gave instructions, she wrote letters, she encoded and decoded notices and messages. Nearly always her room held that faint smell of paper warmed up over a flame. And how often did she complain with her soft insistence that people did not write enough, or that someone made mistakes in the code, or wrote in chemical ink in such a way that one line was blurred by the next, and so on. Even more important, of course, is the fact that in this organizational work at Lenin's side she could day after day observe all that occurred to him and around him. Nonetheless, I hope that my remarks will not prove valueless, especially because Nadezhda Konstantinovna very rarely was present at our staff meetings, at least during my time; but mainly because it may happen that the fresh eye of an outsider notices what more familiar eyes might miss. Be that as it may, what I have narrated I have narrated. And now I should like to make a few general remarks. I am chiefly interested in explaining why, in my view, precisely during the period of the old *Iskra* Lenin should have undergone that decisive crisis of his political personality, of his, so to say, political self-evaluation; why this crisis was both inevitable and necessary.

Lenin went abroad a fully mature man of thirty. In Russia, in the circle of students, in the first Social Democratic groupings, in the colonies of deportees, his was the leading role. He could not be unaware of his strength, if only because it was acknowledged by all those who met him and by all those who worked with him. He had left Russia with a considerable theoretical knowledge and with a great deal of political experience—all this was permeated through and through by that powerful striving toward *the* goal so characteristic of his mental makeup. Abroad he had to collaborate with the group of *The Emancipation of Labor* and first of all with Plekhanov, that profound and brilliant interpreter of Marx, the theoretician, the politician, the publicist, the orator of European fame with European connections from whom so many had learned.

Next to Plekhanov there stood two great authorities: Zasulich and Axelrod. It was not only her heroic past that made of Zasulich a prominent figure; it was her perspicacity, her erudition especially in the field of history, and her exceptional psychological intuition. It was through Zasulich that "The Group" had in the past established relations with the old Engels. In contrast to Plekhanov and Zasulich who had strong links with socialism in the Latin countries, Axelrod represented the idea and the experience of German Social Democracy. This division of "spheres of influence" was reflected also in their places of residence. Plekhanov and Zasulich settled in Geneva, while Axelrod lived in Zurich. Axelrod concentrated on matters of tactics and did not produce theoretical or historical work. Generally speaking, he wrote little, and in his writing he dealt nearly always with the tactical problems of socialism. Here he displayed both originality and shrewdness. From our innumerable conversations—at one time my relations with him and Zasulich were very friendly—I saw clearly that much of Plekhanov's writing on tactical questions was a product of a collective mind, and that Axelrod's contribution was much more weighty than one could deduce from printed documents alone. Axelrod himself used to say to Plekhanov who (till the 1903 split) was the undisputed and beloved chief of "The Group": "You, George, have a long trunk; you'll reach out far for whatever you may need . . ."

Axelrod, as we know, wrote a preface to Lenin's *Tasks of Russian Social Democrats,* which in manuscript form was sent out of Russia. By this act "The Group" had adopted the young talented Russian activist, while at the same time establishing the relations of masters toward the disciple. It was precisely as a disciple that Lenin, with two other comrades, went abroad. I was not present at the first encounters of the pupil with the teachers and at those meetings at which the political line of *Iskra* was being hammered out. It is not difficult, however, in the light of events I have described, and especially in the light of the Second Party Congress, to understand that the very sharpness of the conflict, apart from the differences in principles which only just began to come to the surface, was also caused by the mistaken view the "old" ones took of Lenin's stature and eminence.

During the Second Congress and right after it, the indignation with which Axelrod and the other members of the editorial board criticized Lenin's behavior was mixed with perplexity: "How dare he go that far?" This perplexity increased further, when after the rupture between Plekhanov and Lenin —which occurred very soon after the Congress—Lenin continued the struggle. The frame of mind of Axelrod and the others might perhaps be even better conveyed by the expression *What on earth bit him?* "Not so long ago he left Russia," reasoned the "old" ones, "and came here as a pupil and behaved like one." (This was particularly stressed by Axelrod in what he said about the first months of *Iskra.*) From where this sudden self-confidence? How dare he? Then there were guesses. He had prepared the ground in Russia—not for noth-

ing were the "lines of communication" in the hands of Nadezhda Konstantinovna; it was there that the minds of comrades were being stealthily influenced against the group of
The Emancipation of Labor. Vera Zasulich was no less indignant than others, but perhaps better than they she understood
what was happening. Not without reason did she say about
Lenin, still a long time before the split, that, unlike Plekhanov's, his was a "deadly grip." And who knows what impression these words had made on Lenin at the time? Perhaps he
said to himself, "Yes, this is true. Who understands Plekhanov
better than Vera Zasulich? He shakes and shakes, and then
lets go, and the task is not just to shake and let go . . .
What is needed is the 'deadly grip.' "

To what extent and in what sense it might have been true
that there was some preliminary "working over" of the minds
and opinions of comrades in Russia, Nadezhda Konstantinovna better than anyone else can tell. Even without knowing
all the facts, one can assume that this was broadly true. Lenin
was always preparing for tomorrow, while strengthening and
consolidating what he had gained today. His creative thought
never stood still; his vigilance never flagged. When he became
convinced that *The Emancipation of Labor* group was incapable of providing the immediate leadership of the militant van-
guard of the proletariat in the approaching revolution, he drew
the most practical conclusions. The "old" members of the organization—and not only they—were mistaken. This was no
longer the young and remarkable activist, whose work Axelrod
introduced by providing it with a friendly patronizing preface
—this was a leader totally geared to one purpose; and it
seemed that he grew conscious of being a leader when acting
side by side with his elders; he realized that he was stronger
and more indispensable than they.

True, according to Martov, Lenin was already *primus inter
pares* in Russia. But there he still acted in narrow Social
Democratic circles, in newly formed organizations. Russian

party-men still bore a stamp of parochialism. How many Las-salles did they have; how many Bebels? The stature of *The Emancipation of Labor* group was quite different. Plekhanov, Axelrod, and Zasulich were on a level equal to that of Kaut-sky, Lafargue, Guesde, and Bebel—the real German Bebel! Lenin applied the great European scale when he measured his forces against theirs. It was precisely in the disputes with Plekhanov, when the editorial board was divided into two camps, that Lenin was acquiring that firmness and self-con-fidence without which he would not have become the Lenin of the future. The disagreements with the "old" members were unavoidable, not because there were *a priori* two conceptions of a revolutionary movement—at that time this was not so; what divided them was a different approach to political events, to practical and to organizational questions, and, in conse-quence, they arrived at a different vision of the coming revolu-tion. The old members had already been emigrés for twenty years. For them *Iskra* and *Zaria* were, first and foremost, a literary enterprise, while for Lenin the two publications con-stituted an immediately valuable instrument of revolutionary action. Somewhere deep in Plekhanov there was hidden the revolution's skeptic. This came to the surface later, in 1905 and 1906, and even more tragically during the imperialist war. He was looking down upon Lenin's typically characteristic concentration on the one and unique goal, and had up his sleeve quite a few condescending and malicious jokes about it.

Axelrod, as we have seen, was more preoccupied with tacti-cal problems, but his mind stubbornly refused to move beyond preliminaries to the preparatory. Very often Axelrod displayed considerable art in analyzing tendencies and nuances which characterized particular groups of revolutionary intelligentsia. He was a homeopath of prerevolutionary politics. He applied the procedures and methods of a laboratory; he dealt with minute quantities; he observed the smallest groups; he weighed everything on a chemist's scale. Not for nothing did L. G.

Deutsch consider Axelrod as belonging to the same type as Spinoza. It was not without significance that Spinoza was a diamond cutter—this job, as we know, requires a magnifying glass. Lenin, to the contrary, saw the vast scale of events and relationships, trained his mind to reach to the depth of social masses, and that enabled him to react to the approaching revolution which caught Plekhanov and Axelrod unawares.

Vera Zasulich, it seemed, felt more directly the imminence of the revolution than all the other old members of *Iskra*. Her understanding of history—lively, devoid of pedantry, and shot through with intuition—helped her greatly. But her vision of the revolution was that of an old radical. In the depth of her soul she was convinced that we already had all the elements of the revolution with the exception of the "true" self-confident liberalism which should be the leading force. She was of the opinion that we, Marxists, by our untimely criticism of the liberals and by our "baiting" of them, were really playing a counterrevolutionary role. True, she never expressed such views publicly; even in personal conversations she was rarely outspoken, but nevertheless these were her innermost thoughts. From these thoughts stemmed her antagonism to Paul Axelrod whom she considered a doctrinaire. Indeed, within the limits of his laboratory tactics he invariably insisted on the dominant role of Social Democracy. He refused to transfer the application of his doctrine from groupings and circles to social classes just when social classes were on the move. This was the gulf that separated him from Lenin.

Lenin went abroad neither as a Marxist "generally speaking," nor in order to devote himself to some "general" literary-revolutionary work, nor for the purpose of carrying on the twenty-year-old activities of *The Emancipation of Labor*. No, he came as a potential leader, as *the* leader of the revolution which he sensed and perceived was welling up. He came in order to build, in the shortest possible time, an ideological base and organizational framework for that revolution. When

I spoke about Lenin's tense concentration on his goal—concentration which was both passionate and disciplined—I did not see it as an effort to achieve a "final triumph"—no, that would have been too vague and meaningless—but I saw it as a concrete, direct, immediate work toward the practical aim of speeding the outbreak of the revolution and of securing its victory.

When Lenin, in his activities abroad, found himself side by side with Plekhanov and when there was no longer between them what the Germans call "the impressiveness of distance," it became quite clear to the "pupil" that in matters that were absolutely essential, he, the pupil, not only had almost nothing to learn from the masters, but that the masters by their procrastination and skepticism could hinder the work needed to be done and, because of their authority, could also deflect from it younger collaborators. Hence Lenin's farsighted preoccupation with the editorial team; hence his combinations of "the seven" and "the three"; hence the endeavor to separate Plekhanov from *The Emancipation of Labor* group, to form the leading triumvirate in which Plekhanov would still have a say on the subject of revolutionary theory and Martov on that of revolutionary politics. Personal alliances may be altered, but the bare bones of the plan for the future remained unchanged and finally were clothed with sinew, flesh, and blood.

At the Second Congress Lenin won over Plekhanov, but without hope of retaining him for long. At the same time he lost Martov, and lost him for good. Plekhanov must have sensed something during the Congress. To Axelrod, who reproached him bitterly for his amazing alliance with Lenin, he answered, "From such stuff Robespierres are made." Was this significant remark ever published? Has it been at all known in the party? Anyhow, I guarantee its authenticity. "From such stuff Robespierres are made!" "And even something much greater, George Valentinovich," was history's answer. But evidently this historical discovery faded very quickly in Plekhanov's own consciousness. He broke with Lenin and returned to his skepticism and to the jokes which, incidentally, with the passage of time were losing some of their sting.

In the split, which was already casting its shadow, it was not only Plekhanov and not only the problem of the old members that played a role. The Second Congress in general marked the end of the first, the preliminary stage of the preparatory period. The mere fact that the *Iskra* organization quite unexpectedly became divided into two more or less equal groupings, was in itself a proof that at that stage many problems were as yet unresolved. The conception of a party based on a social class was only just dawning upon the consciousness of intellectual radicals. The flow of the intelligentsia toward Marxism was still continuing. The student movement, at least its left wing, was being attracted to *Iskra*. Among intelligent young people, especially abroad, there were many groups forming which declared their support for *Iskra*. All this was still very youthful, very immature, and, on the whole, rather unstable. At meetings female students asked questions such as "Should a girl, an adherent of *Iskra,* marry a naval officer?" Only three workers took part in the Congress, and they were brought in not without some trouble. On the one hand *Iskra* was recruiting and training professional revolutionary cadres and attracting young and idealistic workers. On the other hand, a considerable number of intellectuals were "passing through" *Iskra* and then transforming themselves into adherents of *Osvobozhdenia*.[9]

Iskra was successful not only as a Marxist organ of an emerging proletarian party, but also as a highly articulate militant political journal of extreme left views. The most radical elements among the intelligentsia were, on the spur of the moment, ready to fight for liberty under the banner of *Iskra*; however, with their didactic-progressive frame of mind, they remained distrustful of the proletariat. Previously this distrust

[9] *See* footnote 5, page 42.

found its expression in "economism"; later it took on, almost ingenuously, the protective coloring of *Iskra* without undergoing any fundamental change. In the final reckoning it was clear that the real conquests of *Iskra* were much less impressive than its brilliant victory. How far Lenin was aware of this fact before the Second Congress, I would not undertake to say now; but undoubtedly it was clearer and more evident to him than to anybody else. Among all these varied tendencies and attitudes assembled under the banner of *Iskra* which found their reflection in the editorial team, Lenin was the only one to personify the future: its grave tasks, its cruel struggles and innumerable victims. Hence the vigilance and suspiciousness of a combatant. Hence his precision in dealing with matters of organization which found its symbolic expression in the famous Paragraph 1 (of the Statutes) determining the membership of the party. It was quite natural therefore that at the Second Congress which was getting ready to gather the fruits of the ideological victories of *Iskra,* Lenin began the task of sifting the cadres anew in a more stern and exacting manner. To take such a step facing the opposition of half the assembly, having Plekhanov as a doubtful semi-ally and all the other members of the editorial staff as determined opponents; to embark in such conditions on a work like this, one had to have faith not only in the cause but also in one's own strength.

This faith in his own strength was the result of Lenin's self-evaluation tested in practical experience. He acquired it during the work with the "masters" and through the first skirmishes—even then there were sparks flying and flashes of lightning portending the thunders and the tempests of the coming rupture. It was Lenin's impressive singleness of purpose which allowed him to embark upon his task and to conclude it. Tirelessly, he was tightening the string of his bow more and more, to the limit—quietly testing: Was there no flaw? No danger that it would snap? From all sides he heard warnings: Do not make it any tauter, don't!

"It will not snap," answered the master archer. "Our bow is made of unbreakable proletarian material, and the string has to be tightened more and more, for the arrow is heavy and we have to launch it far, very far into the distance."

March 5, 1924

II. The Revolution

11 The Revolution

1. On the Eve

AT Amherst, in the Canadian prisoners-of-war camp, I learned from American newspapers that Lenin had returned to Petersburg, was addressing meetings of workers and attacking the war and the Provisional Government. The German sailors, interned with me, were greatly interested in Lenin, whose name they read for the first time in press dispatches. My fellow internees looked forward with great impatience to the end of hostilities which would open for them the gates of their prison. They listened with considerable attention to any voice raised against the war. Up to now they had heard only about Liebknecht; but they had always been told that he sold himself to the enemy. Now they came across Lenin's name. Soon I was telling them about what had happened in Zimmerwald and at Kienthal; Lenin's antiwar activity made many of them recall the ideas of Liebknecht.

Passing through Finland, I first saw recent Russian newspapers. They announced that Tseretelli, Skobelev, and other "socialists" had entered the Provisional Government. This made the situation absolutely clear. On the second or third day after I reached Petersburg, I read Lenin's "April Theses." This was just what the revolution needed. Only later did I see in *Pravda* his article "First Stage of the First Revolution," which he had sent from Switzerland.

The old prerevolutionary copies of *Pravda* should be reread

even now, for they are extremely interesting and politically illuminating. Against a great deal of confused writing, Lenin's
"Letters from Afar" stand out in all their intensity and concentration. His dispassionate theoretical exposition brings to mind
a powerful, tightly wound coil of steel later to unwind, expand,
and encompass the whole ideology of the revolution.

I arranged with Comrade Kamenev to meet the editors of
Pravda a few days after my return. I think I went to see them
on May 5 or 6. I told Lenin that I was in complete agreement
with his "April Theses" and with the whole course which the
party had taken since his arrival, and that I saw before me two
possibilities: either to join the party on my own—"individually"—or to attempt to bring into it the best of the "Unity
Group," who in Petersburg alone numbered 3,000 workers
including a whole pleiad of inestimable revolutionaries like
Uritsky, Lunacharsky, Yoffe, Vladimirov, Manuilsky, Kara-
khan, Yureniev, Posern, Litkens, and others.[1]

At that time Antonov-Ovseenko had already joined the
Party; so had Sokolnikov, if I am not mistaken. Lenin categorically declared himself for neither solution: First of all one
had to acquire more concrete knowledge of the situation and
of the people involved. He did not exclude the possibility of
cooperation with Martov and, generally speaking, with some
of the Mensheviks-Internationalists who had just returned
from abroad; one also had to find out what the collaboration
of the "Internationalists" would look like in practice.

Meeting with Lenin's tacit and general approval, I refrained
from forcing the course of events. We had a common policy.
From the very first day of my arrival in Petersburg when I addressed soldiers' meetings, I used the expression "We, Bolsheviks and Internationalists." As the "and" proved only to hinder
the flow of my arguments, I dropped it and shortened the sen-

[1] *Translator's note:* Trotsky speaks here about the Inter-Borough Organization, the *Mezhrayonka,* of which he was the leader.

tence: "We, Bolsheviks-Internationalists." In such a way our political union preceded the organizational one.[2]

Before the July Days I visited the editorial offices of *Pravda* perhaps twice or three times—always at some very critical juncture.[3] During those first meetings, and even more so after the July Days, Lenin invariably seemed extremely preoccupied —under the apparent calmness and his usual matter-of-fact behavior one could sense a tremendous inner tension. At that time the Kerensky regime seemed all-powerful. Bolshevism seemed a *quantité négligeable*. The party itself was not yet aware of its gathering strength. And yet Lenin was leading it, unfalteringly, toward momentous tasks . . .

His speeches at the First Congress of the Soviets surprised the Social Revolutionary and the Menshevik majority and provoked their anxiety. Confused, they sensed that this man was aiming very, very high. But they did not see his goal. And the *petit bourgeois* revolutionaries wondered: What is he? Who is he? Simply a madman or a historical missile endowed with an unheard-of explosive force?

Lenin's address to the Congress of the Soviets, in which he spoke about the necessity of arresting fifty capitalists, was not perhaps a success from an oratorical point of view. Yet it was of exceptional significance. The short applause of the few Bolsheviks present accompanied the speaker leaving the rostrum. He gave the impression of someone who had not as yet said all he had to say, or who said it not quite as he wished to . . . At that moment an extraordinary breath of air drifted over the hall. It was the blast of the wind of future change felt by everybody, while bewildered eyes anxiously followed Lenin's figure, so ordinary and so enigmatic.

[2] N. N. Sukhanov in *The Russian Revolution—1917* construes my line as differing from that of Lenin. But then Sukhanov is known as a "constructivist."

[3] *Translator's note:* July Days—premature, spontaneous, and abortive semi-insurrection after which severe reprisals followed.

What is this? Who is he? Had not Plekhanov described, in his own paper, Lenin's first speech in revolutionary Petersburg as sheer folly? Was it not clear that the delegates with a mandate from the people were, nearly all of them, joining either the Social Revolutionaries or the Mensheviks? And at times even among the Bolsheviks had not Lenin's position provoked violent disagreement?

On the one hand Lenin demanded a definite break not only with bourgeois liberalism, but also with the partisans of "national defense" no matter what their political complexion. He organized a struggle within his own party against those "old Bolsheviks" who, as he wrote, "have more than once played so grievous a role in the history of our party by repeating a formula meaninglessly *learned by rote,* instead of *studying* the specific and new features of actual reality." [4]

In this way, it might have seemed that he was weakening his own party. At the same time he declared at the Congress of the Soviets: "It is not true to say that no party exists which is ready to assume power; such a party exists. This is our party." Was there not an enormous contradiction between the position of a "circle of propagandists" who kept their distance from all other groups and this haughty claim to assume power over this vast country shaken to its very foundations? And the Congress of the Soviets was absolutely unable to comprehend what he did want or what he hoped for, this strange man, this cool visionary, who wrote short articles in a small newspaper.

When Lenin, with superb sincerity, which only simpletons took for simplemindedness, declared: "Our party is ready to assume power," there was laughter in the hall. "You can laugh as much as you like," said Lenin. He knew that "he laughs best who laughs last." The French saying appealed to Lenin because he was getting ready to have the last laugh himself. And in a quiet manner he went on proving that, to start with, fifty

[4] *Translator's note: Lenin, Selected Works,* Vol. VI, p. 33, Moscow-London, 1934–37.

or a hundred of the more important millionnaires should be arrested; that people should be told that we consider all capitalists to be robbers and that Tereshchenko was only less clever but in no way better than Miliukov. All these were such terribly, such abominably, naïve ideas! And this representative of a small section of the Soviets, which from time to time gave him little applause, declared, "Are you afraid of taking power? Well, we are prepared to take it." In response, there was, of course, laughter, indulgent and condescending laughter, with just a shade of alarm in it.

Furthermore, as the text of his second speech Lenin chose some extremely plain words from a letter of a peasant: how one should exert more pressure on the bourgeoisie so that it "bursts at the seams," because only then would the war finish, and if we did not exert that pressure, things would go badly. Did this simple, naïve quotation constitute Lenin's whole program? How was one not to remain bewildered? Again some laughter, indulgent and anxious. And indeed, if one were to consider this as a program of a propagandist group, the words "to exert pressure on the bourgeoisie" would not have much weight in themselves. And yet those who at the time were so baffled by Lenin's speech did not realize that he was unerringly interpreting history's growing pressure on the bourgeoisie which would in the end inexorably "burst at the seams." Not without reason had Lenin, last May, explained to Maklakov that "the country of workers and poor peasants was a thousand times more to the left than the Chernovs and the Tseretellis, and a hundred times more to the left than all of us Bolsheviks." [5]

Here was the main source of Lenin's tactics. Through the new but already crumbling democratic surface of things, he was looking deep down into "the country of workers and peasants" ready for the great revolution, with that readiness which it was still impossible to express in political terms. Every

[5] Article in *Pravda*, May 19, 1917.

political party which spoke in the name of the workers and peasants was cheating them. Millions of workers and peasants did not yet know our party, had as yet to find out that it was precisely our party which stood for all they were striving for; on the other hand our party was not yet aware of its own potential strength and for this reason it was "a hundred times" more to the right than were the workers and the peasants. What was needed was a two-way exchange: The masses had to discover our party; the party in its turn had to discover the masses. One had to beware of running too much in advance; one had to beware of lagging behind; the task was to enlighten patiently and with perseverance; to explain even what seemed very simple: "Down with the ten capitalist ministers!" The Mensheviks do not agree? Then "down with the Mensheviks!" They laugh? Let them: They will not laugh long; we shall see who will be the last to laugh.

I had put forward a proposal that the Congress should discuss urgently the problem of the new military offensive which was being prepared at the front. Lenin, I remember, approved of my suggestion, but he wanted to discuss it first with the other members of the Central Committee. Comrade Kamenev brought to the session Lenin's hastily sketched Bolshevik resolution concerning the offensive. I do not know whether this document still exists. The text, however, proved for one reason or another unacceptable to both the Bolsheviks and Internationalists. Posern, who was charged with presenting the resolution, also found it inadequate. I drafted a different text which was agreed on and finally presented to the Congress. Our intervention was, if I am not mistaken, directed by Sverdlov whom I met for the first time during this Congress. He was then presiding over the Bolshevik faction.

Sverdlov was so small and so frail that one would have thought he was ill; yet there was something in him which gave the impression of authority and quiet strength. He presided over the discussion without raising his voice, without interrupting the speakers; he worked evenly and smoothly like a well-oiled machine. The secret of his success lay not in his talent for conducting the debate, but in the fact that he was extremely well acquainted with those present in the hall and also that he knew exactly what he was trying to achieve. Before each conference he would meet every delegate individually, would question him and sometimes also brief him. Even before he opened the conference, he had a more or less clear general idea of the turn the discussion would take. But even without the preliminary conversations he knew better than anybody else in what way this or that party worker would react to every particular problem. The number of our comrades with whose political personalities Sverdlov was well acquainted was quite considerable, if one applies the standards of that time. He was a born organizer and planner. He saw every political problem first of all in the light of its intrinsic meaning for the party organization. He saw immediately how particular people and particular groups would react to it and how the alignments inside the organization would shape themselves and what consequently would be the relationship between the party and the masses outside the organization. Almost automatically he was translating algebraic formulas into arithmetical realities. He was able to check the worth of important political slogans against revolutionary actuality.

After the demonstration of June 10 was banned, when the temperature at the First Congress of the Soviets was rising extremely and Tseretelli threatened to disarm the Petersburg workers, I went with Comrade Kamenev to the editorial offices of *Pravda*. After a brief exchange of views, I wrote, at Lenin's suggestion, a draft of an address for the Central Committee to the Executive Committee.

At the offices of *Pravda* Lenin commented in a few words on Tseretelli's last speech, that of June 11. "But he really was a revolutionary once—doing so many years of hard labor! And now this complete renunciation of his past." There was nothing political in that remark, nothing polemical; it was a passing reflection on the sad fate of a former heroic revolutionary. There was a tinge of sorrow and resentment in Lenin's tone, although he spoke curtly and dryly, because nothing was more distasteful to him than a show of sentimentality or psychological ratiocination.

On July 4 or 5 I saw Lenin (and Zinoviev?) at the Taurida Palace, I think. The offensive was repelled. The anti-Bolshevik fury of the ruling group was at its height. "Now they will shoot us all," said Lenin, "for them it is the best moment." Basically, his plan was to beat a retreat and, if necessary, to descend into illegality. This was one of those sharp turns in Lenin's strategy which followed, as usual, upon a rapid assessment of circumstances. Later on, at the time of the Third Congress of the Comintern, Lenin once said, "In July we committed not a few silly blunders." What he meant was that military action had been premature and that our demonstration had taken much too aggressive a form, if one measured our forces against the vastness of the country. All the more remarkable was the sober restraint with which Lenin viewed, on July 4 or 5, the chances not only of revolution but also of its adversaries, for whom, he concluded, had come the best moment to shoot us all. Fortunately, our enemies possessed neither such logical acuteness nor such determination. They were satisfied with chemical concoctions *à la* Perevertzev.[6] However, it was quite probable that if they had succeeded, immediately after the July demonstration, in laying their hands on Lenin, they, or rather their officers, would have done with him what less than two years later German *Soldateska* did with Liebknecht and Rosa Luxemburg.

During our meeting mentioned above no clear decision to hide or to return to secrecy was taken. The Kornilov revolt

[6] *Translator's note:* Perevertzev was the Minister of Justice in Prince Lvov's Provisional Government. He was instrumental in putting into circulation the slanderous accusation which alleged that Lenin was in the service of the German General Staff.

was only gradually taking shape. I myself remained "in evidence" for another two or three days. At a few meetings of the party and of the organization I spoke on the subject: "What is to be done?" Wild attacks on the Bolsheviks seemed irresistible. The Mensheviks tried by all means to take advantage of the situation which had arisen not without their assistance. I remember I had to speak in the Library of the Taurida Palace at a meeting of some representatives of professional trade unions. The top leaders only—in all a few dozen people—were present. The Mensheviks predominated. I kept on stressing how necessary it was for the professional trade unions to protest against the accusation of alleged Bolshevik links with German militarism. I now remember vaguely the course of this meeting, but I have still before me very clearly two or three spiteful faces as if begging to be slapped . . .

In the meantime terror was growing and arrests multiplied. I spent a few days hiding in the flat of Comrade Larin. Then I started going out; I put in an appearance at the Taurida Palace, and soon I was arrested. I was released only during the "Kornilov days" when the Bolshevik wave was mounting. By that time the Inter-Borough Organization had already joined the Bolshevik Party. Sverdlov proposed that I should meet Lenin who was still in hiding. I do not remember who took me (was it Rakhia?) to a worker's lodging which had become Lenin's hiding place. There I also met Kalinin, whom Lenin continued, in my presence, to subject to thorough questioning: What was the mood of the workers? Would they fight? Would they fight to the end? Could we seize power? And so on, and on.

What was Lenin's state of mind at that time? If I were to describe it in a few words, I would say that it was one of controlled impatience and deep anxiety. He saw clearly that the moment was approaching when all would be at stake; at the same time he thought, not unreasonably, that the leadership of the party did not draw from this all the necessary conclusions.

The attitude of the Central Committee was, according to him, too passive; they were waiting for something to turn up. He considered that for him it was impossible to return to work in the open; he rightly feared that if he were arrested, the wait-and-see attitude of the top leadership would become strengthened and even more fixed; this would unavoidably have led us to miss the exceptional revolutionary situation. Hence Lenin's extreme vigilance. During these days and weeks his denunciations of any sign of opportunism or procrastination and irresolution grew sharper and more violent than ever.

He demanded that a cabal should be organized immediately: the enemy caught unawares; power seized; and then, we shall see . . . However, all this I shall have to describe in more detail.

The biographer will have to consider with the greatest attention the question of Lenin's return to Russia and the way in which he came into contact with the Russian masses. Apart from a short period in 1905, Lenin had spent fifteen years as an emigré abroad. His sense of the real, his intimate understanding of the living and toiling worker, had not at all weakened during these years; on the contrary, through theoretical study and his creative imagination it had become even more solid. From episodic and accidental encounters, from observation whenever an opportunity occurred, Lenin gathered details which allowed him to build a whole.

However, it was as an emigré that he spent those years of his life during which he finally acquired the stature to play his future historical role. When he arrived in Petersburg, he brought with him those revolutionary conclusions which summed up all his social-theoretical work and all the practical experience of his life. He proclaimed the watchword of socialist revolution the minute he touched the soil of Russia. But only then, face to face with the awakening working masses of Russia, did the practical trial of all the accumulated knowl-

edge, all that had been pondered, and all that had been re-
solved begin. The formulas stood the test. Moreover, here in
Russia, in Petersburg, in daily life, the formulas took a concrete irrefutable shape and consequently an irresistible force.
Now there was no need to construe the image of the whole
from fragments gathered more or less accidentally. The entire reality asserted itself with the full voice of the revolution.
And here Lenin demonstrated—or perhaps he himself realized
it fully for the first time—to what a degree his ear was attuned
to the still discordant clamor of the awakening masses. With
what profound, almost organic, contempt he viewed the mouse-
like scurrying of the leading parties of the February revolution, and the waves of "powerful" public opinion beating upon
one newspaper and another; with what scorn he looked at the
shortsighted, self-satisfied, babbling officials of the Russia of
the February days! Behind this stage hung with democratic
props, he heard the rumble of events on quite a different scale.
When the skeptics were pointing to all the difficulties of his
enterprise, to the mobilization of bourgeois public opinion, to
the simplicity of the *petit bourgeois*—he set his teeth, his
muscles tense across his high cheekbones. This meant that he
was restraining himself so as not to tell the skeptics plainly
and bluntly what he thought of them. He saw and he understood the difficulties just as well as did the others; but he also
had the almost physical awareness—as if it were tangible—of
the gigantic historical forces pent up and now ready for the
tremendous burst which was to overcome all obstacles. He
saw, heard, and understood, in the first instance, the Russian
workers whose numbers grew, who had not forgotten the
events of 1905, who had gone through the school of war with
all its illusions, through the falsehood and lies of the "defense
of the nation," and were now prepared for the greatest sacrifices and unprecedented efforts. He understood the soldier who,
stunned by three years of senseless and absurd carnage, was

now stirred by the thunder of revolution and was preparing to pay for all the needless sufferings, all the humiliations and blows with an outburst of hatred, sparing nobody.

He guessed the mood of the peasants, who, still trailing behind them the chains of centuries of serfdom, now in the turmoil of war, for the first time saw the chance of settling scores with the oppressors, the exploiters, the landlords, and the masters. The *muzhik* was still helplessly shuffling along, wavering between the empty verbiage of Chernov and the old "method" of agrarian revolt. The soldier was still dragging his feet looking for a way out between patriotism and foolish desertions. The workers were still half-listening, but with distrust and some hostility, to the last tirades of Tseretelli. The steam in the boilers of the Kronstadt warships was already hissing impatiently.

The sailor who had in himself all the hatreds of the worker, as sharp as a steel blade, and all the heavy bearlike wrath of the *muzhik,* this sailor, singed by the flames of the terrible war, was already throwing overboard all that in his eyes embodied tyranny: the whole social hierarchy of military and bureaucratic oppressors. The February revolution was on the way out. The rags of legality of the czarist regime were being picked up by a coalition of its saviors, stretching, mending, and patching them into a thin cloak of democratic legitimacy. But underneath, everything was bubbling and boiling, and the old anger was coming to the top. There was the hatred of the bailiff and of the landlord, of the district officer, of the inspector, of the chief of the police, of the manager, of the usurer, of the factory owner, of the parasite, of the "man with white hands," of the despot and the tyrant—this was the prelude to the great revolutionary upheaval. And this was what Lenin heard and what he saw. Immediately after his return to a country which was in the throes of revolution, he sensed all this with his whole being, with an extraordinary acuteness, with an absolute certainty.

"You imbeciles, braggarts, idiots, you think that history is made in drawing rooms where upstart democrats fraternize with titled liberals, where miserable provincial pettifoggers of yesterday learn to kiss the gracious hands of their Eminences! Imbeciles, braggarts, idiots! History is made in the trenches where the soldier, possessed by the nightmare of war-madness, plunges his bayonet into the officer's stomach and then, clinging like grim death to the buffers of a train carriage, escapes to his native village there to set fire to his landlord's manor. You don't like this brutality? 'Don't get cross,' answers history: 'You are treated to all that I possess. What happens now is simply the result of what went on before.' Do you truly imagine that history is made in your 'contact commissions'? Nonsense, childish prattle, tomfoolery, stupidity. History—as all will soon see—this time has chosen as its workshop-laboratory the palace of Kshesinskaya, the ballerina, the one-time mistress of the former czar. Here, in this edifice, so symbolic of the old Russia, history prepares the liquidation of our monarchical, bureaucratic, courtly, landed, and bourgeois corruption and squalor. To this palace of the former imperial ballerina flock sweaty factory delegates, gray, haggard, and lousy foot-envoys from the trenches and from here they carry throughout the country their prophetic message."

Woeful ministers of the revolution deliberated and meditated on how to give back the palace to its rightful owner. The newspapers of the Social Revolutionaries, of the Mensheviks, of the bourgeois parties were gnashing their rotten teeth, because from the balcony of the Kshesinskaya Palace Lenin's call for social upheaval was resounding. But their belated efforts could neither increase Lenin's hatred of the old Russia nor strengthen his will to settle accounts with her. Both his hatred and his will reached their final limit. On the Kshesinskaya balcony stood Lenin, the same man who two months later would be hiding in a hayloft; and, after that, in a few weeks at most, would become the Chairman of the People's Commissars.

At the same time Lenin saw that within the party itself there was conservative opposition (at first not so much political as psychological) to the great leap which now had to be made. Lenin watched with anxiety the growing divergence between the mood of some leaders and that of the working masses. His apprehension was not allayed by the fact that the Central Committee adopted the formula of armed uprisings. He knew all the difficulties of passing from words to deeds. Persistently and by all means available to him, he worked to subject the party to the pressure of the masses and the Central Committee; to the pressure of the rank and file of the party. At the same time he was acutely aware that there was no time to be lost. It is impossible to maintain a revolutionary situation at will until such moment as the party is ready to make use of it. This we have learned recently from the German experience. Not so long ago some people had argued: If we had not seized power in October, we would have seized it two or three months later. This is a profoundly mistaken view. Had we not seized power in October, we would not have seized it at all. Before October our strength lay precisely in the fact that the masses were pouring into our party because they believed that *it* would do what others had failed to do. If the working classes had detected in us the slightest sign of vacillation, of hesitation, or of a divergence between our words and our deeds, within two or three months the tide would have ebbed away just as it ebbed away from the SR's and the Mensheviks. The bourgeoisie would have obtained a respite and would have used it for concluding the peace. The whole relation of forces would have been radically changed and the proletarian upheaval would have been postponed indefinitely. Lenin understood, sensed, and felt this; hence his anxiety and fear, his distrust, and his frantic pressure saved the revolution.

The dissensions within the party which came violently to

the surface during the days of October had previously made their appearance at various stages of the revolution. The first conflict over principles was still conducted in the calm manner in which theoretical questions are debated. It arose immediately after Lenin's return to Russia in connection with his "April Theses." A little later the dull thud of the second clash was heard: Here was the question of the demonstration of armed workers on April 20. The third disagreement arose over the armed demonstration of June 10. The "moderates" maintained that Lenin schemed to implicate them in a demonstration which would have led to an armed rising. The next conflict, a much sharper one, occurred as a result of the July Days.

This time the disagreements were reported by the newspapers. The problem of the Pre-Parliament became another subject of inner-party struggle in which two openly contesting groups stood face to face. Were any minutes made during the party session? Has any report of it been preserved? The discussions were undoubtedly of tremendous interest. Two distinct factions made their appearance: one demanding the seizure of power; the other determined to enter the Constituent Assembly and there to play the role of opposition. Those who were against participation in the Pre-Parliament were in a minority, though the majority of the other group was not very considerable. To the debates and to the final decision Lenin reacted immediately. From his hiding place he wrote to the Central Committee, expressing with great vigor his solidarity with those who refused to enter the Bulygin Duma—the Pre-Parliament of Kerensky and Tseretelli. I did not find this letter in the second part of Volume XIV of Lenin's *Works*. Has this extremely valuable document been preserved? [7]

The dissensions reached their climax immediately before October when the party was finally to enter the road of revolution and fix the date of the uprising. Later, after October 25

[7] *Translator's note:* The letter has been published in Lenin's *Sochinenya*, Moscow, 1962, fifth edition, Vol. XXXIV, p. 342.

(November 7 in the new calendar), the tension became even sharper when the problem of the coalition with other socialist parties was debated.

It would be highly interesting to reconstruct in all its concrete details Lenin's role on the eve of April 20, of June 10, and just before the July Days. "In July we committed a lot of blunders," Lenin used to say later, not only in private conversations but also at meetings with the German delegates after the March uprising of 1921 in Germany. What were these "blunders"? Energetic, perhaps too energetic experiments; trying to find hastily, perhaps too hastily, how far we could press forward. From time to time this kind of reconnoitering was necessary, otherwise we would have lost contact with the masses. On the other hand, it is well known that scouts too far in advance may sometimes—whether one wants it or not—involve one in a major battle. This did not happen in July. The retreat was sounded in time. Furthermore, the enemy lacked the courage to commit themselves. This was no matter of chance; the Kerensky regime in its very essence was a regime of half-measures; this craven Kerenskyism successfully paralyzed the adventurer Kornilov.

2. *The Uprising*

The date of the Second Congress of the Soviets was set, at our insistence, to coincide with the end of the Democratic Conference, that is, October 25. In view of the fever of agitation which was mounting from hour to hour not only in the workers' districts but also in the soldiers' barracks, it seemed to us that it would be most expedient to focus the attention of the

Petersburg garrison on that particular day on which the Congress of the Soviets would have to decide the question of the seizure of power. The workers and the soldiers, being properly prepared for this, would proclaim their support for the Congress. Our strategy was, in fact, an offensive one. We moved to win power, but our propaganda was based on the assumption that our enemies were intent on dispersing the Congress of the Soviets and therefore had to be repulsed ruthlessly. In this plan we relied on the powerful tide of revolution which was rising everywhere and thus allowing the enemy no respite and no repose. Even the most backward regiments remained, at least, neutral. In such conditions the government's slightest move against the Petrograd Soviet would have immediately assured our decisive preponderance. Lenin, however, feared that our adversary might succeed in bringing in a small but resolutely counterrevolutionary number of troops, might attack first and in this way gain the advantage of surprise. By catching the Party and the Soviet off their guard, by arresting the top leaders in Petrograd, the enemy would decapitate the whole movement and then, gradually, render it powerless. "We dare not wait, we dare not delay," urged Lenin.

Such was the situation when at the end of September or in the beginning of October the now-famous night session of the Central Committee took place in the Sukhanovs' flat. This time Lenin arrived absolutely determined to carry through such a resolution as to leave no room for doubt, vacillation, procrastination, passivity, or delay.

Moreover, even before he had taken his stand against the opponents of the armed uprising, he rebuked those who connected the uprising with the Second Congress of the Soviets. Somebody told him that I said "We have already fixed the date of the rising for October 25." I had indeed repeatedly said this, when I argued against those comrades who saw the road of revolution leading through Pre-Parliament and through "impressive" Bolshevik opposition in the Constituent

Assembly. "If the Congress of the Soviets, where the Bolsheviks are in a majority, will not take power," I maintained, "then Bolshevism, as a whole, will have to pay a heavy price for this. In that case the Constituent Assembly will probably not be convened at all. By the mere fact that after all that had happened, we did convene the October 25 Congress of the Soviets which, we knew beforehand, had an assured Bolshevik majority, we publicly pledged ourselves to seize power not later than on that date."

Vladimir Ilyich protested violently. The question of the Second Congress of the Soviets, he said, was of no interest to him: What importance had it at all? Would the Congress take place? And suppose that it did take place, what would follow? We had to win power and not to tie ourselves to the Congress. It was ridiculous and absurd to warn the enemy about the date of the rising. At best, the date of October 25 could be used to hoodwink the enemy, but it was imperative that the rising should break out sooner and independently of the Congress. First the Party must seize power, arms in hand, and then we could talk about the Congress. We should pass over to action immediately.

As in the July Days, when Lenin definitely expected that "they" would shoot us all, so now he analyzed the whole situation from the point of view of our enemies. The bourgeoisie would gain most if they attacked us suddenly, disrupting the revolution and then finishing it off bit by bit. As in July, Lenin overrated both the shrewdness and the vigor—and perhaps the material possibilities too—of our opponents. To some degree, Lenin's appraisal of the enemy had a purpose which was tactically correct: By overestimating the enemy's forces, he aimed at stimulating the party and provoking it to redouble its efforts.

And yet the party could not seize power by itself, independently of the Soviets and behind its back. This would have been a mistake, the consequences of which would have affected the attitude of the workers and might have had harmful repercussions within the Petersburg garrison. The soldiers knew their delegates in the Soviet; it was through the Soviet that they knew the party. If the uprising had taken place behind the back of the Soviet, independent of it, without its authority and not openly and for all to see as a further step in the struggle for power, there might have been a dangerous confusion among the troops. Besides, one should not forget that in Petersburg, side by side with the local Soviet, there still existed the old All-Russian Central Executive Committee at the head of which stood the SR's and the Mensheviks. Only the Congress of the Soviets could be set against this Committee.

After all, in the Central Committee itself there existed three distinct factions: first, those who opposed the seizure of power and whose logic of the situation led them to reject the slogan "all power to the Soviets"; second, Lenin, who demanded the immediate organization of the uprising, independently of the Soviets; and third, those who considered it imperative to link the uprising closely with the Second Congress of the Soviets so that even the date of the two events should coincide. "In any case," insisted Lenin, "the uprising must precede the Congress, otherwise they will disperse you and you will have no chance to convene the Congress." Finally, according to the proposed resolution, the uprising was to take place not later than October 15. About this, as far as I remember, there was hardly any discussion. Everybody understood that this was an approximate date, a point of time, which could, according to circumstances, be advanced or delayed, but only for a matter of days. The need for a "deadline," and a close one at that, was absolutely clear.

The main debates at the sessions of the Central Committee were, of course, devoted to the struggle against the faction which opposed armed uprising altogether. I would not undertake to reproduce here Lenin's three or four interventions during the last session, when he discussed the following questions:

Should we seize power? Is it time to seize power? Will we be able to remain in power after the insurrection? At that period and also later Lenin wrote many pamphlets and articles dealing with these problems. His way of reasoning, when he addressed the session, was, of course, the same; it is impossible, however, to convey the general atmosphere, the tenseness of these passionate improvisations permeated through and through with the effort to impart to critics, to the hesitant, to the doubting, his own thought, his own willpower, his own conviction and his courage. The destiny of revolution was in the balance. The meeting ended late at night. Every one of us felt like a patient after a surgical operation. Together with a few comrades I spent the rest of that night in Sukhanov's home.

The further course of events, as is well known, helped us a great deal. The attempt to disband the local garrison resulted in the formation of a revolutionary war committee. Now we were in a position to "legalize" our preliminaries for the uprising, to back them by the authority of the Soviet, and also to show how vital was our cause for all the troops in Petrograd. In the short spell of time between the session of the Central Committee in Sukhanov's home and October 25 I met Vladimir Ilyich only once, I think, and even this one meeting I recall rather hazily. When was it? It must have been some time between October 15 and October 25. I remember that I was very curious to learn what had been Lenin's reaction to the "defensive" character of the speech I made at the session of the Petrograd Soviet. I had branded as false all the rumors according to which we were preparing an armed uprising for October 22 (which was "The Day of the Proletarian Soviet"); at the same time I had warned that we would meet every attack against us with a merciless and resolute counterattack. When I saw Vladimir Ilyich it struck me that he was in a rather serene and confident mood, and, I would say, he was less suspicious. He not only had nothing critical to say about my speech, he even approved of it, considering its defensive tone useful as a means to lull the vigilance of the enemy. He, nevertheless, kept on shaking his head and asking: "Won't they forestall us? Won't they attack all of a sudden?" I was trying to prove that from now on everything would go on almost automatically. During that conversation, or at least during a part of it, Comrade Stalin was present, if I am not mistaken. It might be, however, that I am here compressing two meetings into one. Generally speaking, I must admit that my recollections of the last few days before the actual upheaval became extremely confused and telescoped in my memory, so that it is difficult for me to sort them out and establish clearly the time and place of every incident.

My next meeting with Lenin occurred on the very day of October 25, at the Smolny Institute. At what time? I have no idea, but it must have been toward evening. I well remember the anxious tone of his first inquiry about the state of negotiations which we were conducting with the General Staff of the Petrograd district concerning the future of the local garrison. The newspapers had just announced that the negotiations were nearing a favorable conclusion. "So you are aiming at a compromise solution, are you?" asked Lenin, his glance piercing us. I answered that we had "leaked" to the newspapers this reassuring piece of news on purpose: this was only a bit of *ruse de guerre*, military cunning, which we used at the very moment we were opening the general battle. "Ah, that's good, good, excellent," he sang out joyfully and gaily; he started vigorously pacing up and down the room, rubbing his hands energetically: "That's ve-ry excellent!" Military stratagems always appealed to him. To deceive the enemy, to make him look foolish—wasn't this a delightful prospect! In this case the cunning maneuver had quite a special significance; it really meant that we had embarked directly upon a decisive course of action. I related to him that our military operations were already well advanced and that several important points of the city were in our hands. Vladimir Ilyich noticed (or perhaps I showed him) a poster printed the day before in which we threatened with summary execution any person caught in the act of plunder or looting during the uprising. At first Lenin seemed disconcerted, even a little doubtful perhaps. But then he said, "Well, that's right." With breathless impatience he kept on inquiring about the smallest details; for him they constituted irrefutable proof that this time the tide of events was irreversible, that the Rubicon had been crossed, that there was no possibility of retreat, no way back. He was, I remember, greatly impressed by the fact that in a written order I called upon the Pavlovsky regiment to secure the safety of the presses in which party and Soviet newspapers were being printed.

"And what, the regiment came out?"

"Yes, it did."

"And the papers are going to be published?"

"Yes, they are."

Lenin was overjoyed; he was cheerful, laughing, rubbing his hands. Then he lapsed into silence, thought for a while, and said, "Oh, all right, one can proceed in this fashion as well, provided we seize power."

I understood that it was only then that he finally made peace with the fact that we were not proceeding by way of a conspiracy and a plot. But till the very end he was apprehensive lest the enemy thwart our plans or attack us, throwing us off balance. Only now, that is on the evening of October 25, he became more composed and gave his definite approval to the manner in which affairs were being conducted. I said that he became "more composed"—but then he immediately started worrying about a whole series of problems, small and not so small, material and less so, connected with the further course of events.

"Listen," he would say, "wouldn't it be better to do this in such a way? Shouldn't we try to do this or that? Wouldn't it be advisable to appeal to so and so? Or call out such and such?"

All these interminable questions and suggestions may have seemed disconnected, but they all had the same source: the intensity of the thought which in one great sweep embraced the totality of the revolution.

One has to learn not to lose one's breath in the rush of revolutionary events. When the tide is flowing strongly, when the forces of the revolution are automatically gathering strength, and the forces of reaction are scattering and fritter away, then there is the great temptation to let oneself be carried by the elemental power of the mighty wave. Too quick a success may be as dangerous as defeat. Not to lose sight of the guideline of events; after each new success to tell oneself: Nothing yet has been achieved, nothing made quite secure; five minutes before final victory to act with the same vigilance, the same energy, and the same tenacity with which one acted five minutes before the beginning of the military operations; five minutes after victory, even before the first triumphant applause has sounded, to remind oneself: What has been conquered has not yet been secured and no time must be lost—such was the attitude, such was the manner and such was the method of Lenin; such was the essence of his political character and revolutionary spirit.

I have already described elsewhere how Dan, going probably to one of the meetings of the Menshevik faction of the Second Congress of the Soviets, recognized Lenin in his disguise. We were sitting with Vladimir Ilyich at a small table in one of the rooms through which people had to pass. This scene has already become a subject of a painting which, however, as far as I can judge from the photographs, in no way conveys the reality of the situation. This, incidentally, applies to all historic paintings, and to other arts as well. I do not remember in what circumstances, but much later I said to Vladimir Ilyich, "One should make a note of this incident, otherwise people will tell lies about it."

He waved his hand in a comic gesture of helplessness. "It doesn't matter—there will be no end to lies anyhow . . ."

Lenin did not take part in the first session of the Second Congress of the Soviets in the big hall of the Smolny Institute. He remained in one of the adjoining rooms, in which, as I remember, there was for some reason very little furniture, or perhaps none at all. Later somebody spread two sheets on the floor and placed two cushions on them. We were both resting, lying down side by side. But after a few minutes I was called.

"Dan is speaking—you have to answer."

After having given my rebuttal to Dan, I went back to lie down again. Vladimir Ilyich did not even think of falling asleep. How could one? Every five or ten minutes somebody would run in from the hall to tell us what was going on there. Apart from this, messengers were arriving from the city where the troops, commanded by Antonov-Ovseenko, were laying siege to the Winter Palace; our assault had to end the siege.

Next morning I think it was, the morning which only a sleepless night separated from the previous day, I glanced at the tired face of Vladimir Ilyich. Smiling, he said, "Too sudden a transition from secrecy and the regime of Perevertzev —to power . . . *Es schwindelt*. 'One gets dizzy.' "

I do not know why he said it in German. He supplemented his words with an eloquent gesture of his hand: round and round his forehead. After this single more or less personal remark we passed on to deal with current affairs.

3. Brest Litovsk

To arouse the masses of Germany, of Austria-Hungary, as well as of the Entente—this was what we hoped to achieve by entering into peace negotiations. Having this aim in mind, we reasoned that the negotiations should drag on as long as possible, in this way giving the European workers enough time to acquire a proper understanding of the actuality of the revolution, and, more especially, of the revolution's policy of peace. After the first breakdown of peace talks, Lenin proposed that I should go to Brest Litovsk. By itself the prospect of talks with Baron Kühlmann and General Hoffmann was hardly attractive, but, as Lenin expressed himself, "in order to temporize, a temporizer is needed." At the Smolny we had briefly exchanged ideas as to the general line of negotiations. The question whether we should sign the peace or not was for the time being postponed: It was impossible to foresee what course the negotiations would take, what effect they would produce in Europe, and what the general situation would be. We had not, of course, given up hope of some swift revolutionary developments.

That we were not in a position to go on fighting was absolutely evident to me. On my way to Brest Litovsk, passing through the front line, I realized that our comrades, regardless of all warnings and exhortations, were quite unable to organize any kind of demonstration against Germany's excessive demands. The trenches were almost empty; nobody dared to utter a word about the continuation of war under any conditions. "Peace, peace, whatever happens!"

Later, after my return from Brest Litovsk, I tried to persuade a representative of the military faction of the All-Russian Central Executive Committee that he should support our delegation by making a "patriotic" speech. "Impossible," he answered, "quite impossible; we would not be able to return to the trenches—nobody would understand us; we would lose all influence . . ." A revolutionary war was impossible—about this there was not the slightest shade of disagreement between Vladimir Ilyich and myself.

The question was: Would the Germans be able to fight, would they be able to launch an attack against a revolution which proclaims the end of hostilities? How to find this out, how to probe the mood of the German masses and of the German soldiers? What impression had the February and then the October revolution made on them? The January strikes in Germany indicated that some upheaval had started. How serious was it? Should one not put the German working classes and the German Army to the test: On the one hand, proletarian revolution proclaiming the end of the war; on the other, the Hohenzollern regime ordering the launching of an offensive against that very revolution.

"Certainly, this is very tempting," objected Lenin, "and no doubt such a test will have its impact. But it's risky, very risky. And German militarism may prove sufficiently powerful to launch an offensive against us—what then? No, we cannot take the risk. At the moment there is nothing more important in the world than our revolution."

The dispersal of the Constituent Assembly at first made our international situation much worse. The Germans had feared that we might come to an understanding with the "patriotic" Constituent Assembly and that this might result in an attempt to continue the war. Such an attempt would have been senseless and would have led to the final defeat both of the revolution and of the country. But this would become obvious only later on; in the meantime the Germans would have had to make one more effort. Did they see the dispersal of the Constituent Assembly as evidence of our readiness to put an end to hostilities at no matter what price?

Kühlmann became immediately more insolent. What would have been the reaction of the working class of the Entente to the dispersal of the Assembly? It was easy to find an answer to this question. The press of the Entente treated the Soviet regime simply as an agency of the Hohenzollerns—there you are: The Bolsheviks disperse the "democratic" Assembly in order to conclude an infamous peace with the Germans just at the time when Belgium and northern France are under German occupation. It was quite clear that the bourgeois press of the West would succeed in spreading terrible confusion among the working classes. This, in turn, would facilitate military intervention against us. It was well-known, even in Germany, that in the circles of the Social Democratic opposition, there were persistent rumors alleging that the Bolsheviks were in the pay of the German government and that what went on at Brest Litovsk was only a comedy in which the roles had been assigned to the actors in advance. How much more credible such a version of events must have seemed to the French and to the English!

I maintained that before we proceeded to sign the peace it was absolutely imperative that we should prove to the workers of Europe, in a most striking manner, how great, how deadly, was our hatred for the rulers of Germany. Precisely these considerations led me, during my stay in Brest Litovsk, to have recourse to an "instructive" presentation of our attitude which was summed up in the formula: We stop the war but do not sign the peace. I consulted the other members of the delegation who gave their assent and I wrote to Vladimir Ilyich. He answered: We shall discuss this when you come back. It is possible that by this kind of answer Lenin actually hinted at his disagreement. I do not remember this clearly at the present moment and I have not his letter at hand—I am not even sure it has been preserved. After my return we had long discussions with Vladimir Ilyich in the Smolny.

"All this is very attractive and one could wish for nothing better, if only General Hoffmann were not strong enough to throw his troops against us. But of this there is little hope. For his purposes he will find hand-picked regiments of rich Bavarian peasants—he does not need many . . . You yourself say that our trenches are deserted. And what if he really renews hostilities?"

"Then we shall be forced to sign the peace, but it will become clear to all that we have no other way out. This by itself will decisively dispose of the legends that we have some behind-the-scenes links with the Hohenzollerns."

"To be sure, there are advantages . . . And yet there are too many risks. There is nothing more important in the world than our revolution; the revolution has to be safeguarded no matter what the price."

To the essential difficulties of the situation were added considerable complications within the party. In the party, or at least among its leading personalities, the dominant mood was one of intransigence: We must reject German conditions and refuse to sign the peace. The reports which our newspapers published about the course of negotiations maintained and sharpened this mood, which found its most striking expression among the left Communists who put forward the slogan of revolutionary war. Lenin, of course, became alarmed by such developments.

"If the Central Committee decides to accept German conditions presented in the form of a verbal ultimatum only, we are running the risk of a split in the party," I argued. "Our party, no less than the workers of Europe, must be made clearly aware of the real state of affairs . . . If we break with the left wing, the party will make a sharp turn to the right: it is a fact that those comrades who were militantly against the October insurrection and for the alliance with socialist parties, are now unreservedly for peace. And the signing of peace is not our only task. Among the left Communists are some of the most active fighters for the revolution . . ."

"All this is undeniable," answered Vladimir Ilyich, "but the fate of the revolution is at stake. We shall reestablish a balance in the party, but, first of all, we must save the revolution, and we can save the revolution only by signing the peace. Better a split in the party than the danger of a military defeat of the revolution. The leftists will cease making trouble, and then—even if they provoke the split, which is by no means certain—they will come back to the party. If the Germans crush us, then there will be nobody to come back . . . All right, suppose that we accept your plan. We have refused to sign the peace, and then the Germans launch an offensive. What do you do then?"

"We sign the peace at the points of their bayonets. The moral of the scene is obvious to the working class of the whole world."

"And then will you not support the slogan of a revolutionary war?"

"Under no circumstances."

"If this is so, then the experiment may not be so very dangerous. We may lose Esthonia and Latvia. Esthonian comrades came to see me and described to me how well they have succeeded in introducing the socialist system in the countryside. It would be a great pity to sacrifice a socialist Esthonia," added Lenin with a smile, "but we may have to; we may have to do this for the sake of peace."

"And if the peace is signed immediately—does this exclude the possibility of German military intervention in Esthonia or Latvia?"

"All right, maybe not. But it is a possibility there, while

here we face a certainty. I, in any case, shall declare myself for immediate peace. This seems more sure."

The main danger which Lenin saw in my plan consisted in this: In case of a new German offensive, we would not be able to sign the peace because German militarism would leave us no time to do so. "German militarism is a beast that moves swiftly," Vladimir Ilyich kept on repeating. At meetings at which the question of peace was debated, Lenin spoke sharply against the left, and with calm and circumspection against my plan. However, he later accepted it though very reluctantly: the party was obviously opposed to the signing of peace, and it was felt that a kind of intermediate decision might constitute a bridge leading toward some compromise solution.

A conference of the most prominent Bolsheviks, that is of the delegates to the Third Congress of the Soviets, showed beyond all doubt that our party, having so recently emerged from the hot furnace of October, had to test itself in the international arena. If there were no intermediate formula, the majority would have pronounced itself for the revolutionary war.

It is perhaps worth noting that the left Social Revolutionaries were not straightway against the Brest Litovsk peace. In any case, Spiridonova was at first decidedly for signing. "The *muzhik* does not want war," she said, "and they will accept any kind of peace."

"Sign the treaty at once," she told me when I first returned from Brest, "and abolish the grain monopoly." Later, on the left, SR's supported the intermediate formula of ending the hostilities without signing any peace; but they considered the formula as a step toward proclaiming the revolutionary war—"in case of need."

We knew that the German representatives received our declaration in a way which suggested that Germany had no intention of renewing the offensive. Such was the conclusion with which we returned to Moscow.

"Won't they cheat us?" Lenin was asking. With an expansive gesture of our hands we meant to indicate that it was rather unlikely.

"Oh, well," said Lenin, "if so that's all to the good. *Les apparences*[1] (appearances) are saved and here we are, out of war." (The conversations in this chapter are not, of course, quoted word for word, but the expression *"les apparences"* I remember literally.)

However, two days before the end of the truce, we received from our General Samoylo, who had remained at Brest, a telegram informing us that according to General Hoffmann's communication, Germany considered itself from midday, February 18, to be in a state of war with us and therefore requested Samoylo to leave Brest Litovsk. The first to receive this telegram was Vladimir Ilyich. I was in his office. We had been talking with Karelin and with another comrade belonging to the left Social Revolutionaries.

Having glanced at the text, Lenin handed it to me without a word. From his expression I immediately guessed that here was an important and grave piece of news. Lenin hastened to end the conversation with the Social Revolutionaries—he wanted to discuss the sudden turn of events.

"In spite of everything, they cheated us. They gained five days . . . This beast will not let a thing go. That means that now there is nothing left but to sign the old conditions, if only the Germans will still stick to them."

I argued that we should let Hoffmann actually go over to the offensive.

"But that means that we shall have to give up Dvinsk, lose a great deal of artillery, and so on?"

"Yes, of course, this means fresh sacrifices. But I think that the German soldier should in fact step onto Soviet territory arms in hand. And this should be made known to the German

[1] *Translator's note:* In French in the original text.

workers on the one side, and to the French and English workers on the other."

"No," contradicted Lenin. "Of course, it is not a matter of Dvinsk. Now not an hour must be wasted. We have made the experiment. Hoffmann wants to fight and is able to fight. Impossible to delay—they have already robbed us of five days which I wanted to make use of. This beast leaps fast."

The Central Committee took the decision to send a telegram expressing our readiness to sign the peace treaty immediately. The telegram was duly dispatched.

"It seems to me," I said to Lenin in a private conversation, "that politically it would be expedient if I resigned as a Commissar for Foreign Affairs."

"What for? We do not want to introduce these Parliamentary procedures here."

"But my resignation would be seen by the Germans as a radical shift in policy; it would strengthen their trust that this time we are really prepared to sign the peace and abide by it."

"That's possible," answered Lenin thoughtfully. "This is a weighty political argument."

I do not remember at what precise moment we received the news about the German invasion of Finland and about the attack on the Finnish workers. I recall that I came across Vladimir Ilyich in the corridor near his office. He was extremely agitated. I have never seen him in such a state, never before nor after.

"Well, well," he said, "it looks as if we have to fight, though we have nothing to fight with. This time, it seems, there is no other way out . . ."

Such was Lenin's first reaction to the news of the defeat of the Finnish revolution. But already ten or fifteen minutes later, when I entered his office, he said, "No, we should not change our policy. Our action would not have saved revolutionary Finland, but without any doubt would have brought our ruin. We shall do whatever we can to help the Finnish workers—but short of war and still maintaining peace. I do not know whether this will still save us now. In any case, this is our only road to salvation."

And indeed salvation came that way.

The refusal to sign the peace treaty was not, as it is now maintained, the result of an abstract idea that any agreement between us and the imperialists was unthinkable. It is enough to consult a pamphlet by Comrade Ovsyannikov, in which he described an extremely illuminating survey conducted by Lenin on this subject. The survey proves convincingly that the partisans of the tentative policy of "neither war nor peace" answered "Yes" to the question whether we, as a revolutionary party, were entitled to sign, in a certain situation, a "shameful" peace. As a matter of fact, we did maintain that if there were only twenty-five chances in a hundred that the Hohenzollerns would decide not to fight, or if they found themselves in no position to fight, we would have to take the risk and make the experiment.

Three years later we took another chance—this one at Lenin's initiative—to sound, with the help of our bayonets, the situation in Poland, the Poland of the bourgeoisie and petty nobility. We were repulsed. What was then the difference between the Polish "sounding" and the Brest Litovsk test? As to the general principle, there was no difference; there was only one in the degree of the risk we took.

I remember that Comrade Radek once wrote that the powerful sweep of Lenin's tactical ideas could best be noticed in the period between the signature of the Brest Litovsk Treaty and the March on Warsaw. Now we all know that the March on Warsaw was a very costly mistake, resulting not only in the conclusion of the Riga Treaty which cut us off from Germany, but also, together with other contemporary developments, it helped tremendously in the consolidation of bourgeois Europe. The counterrevolutionary character of the Riga Treaty and its influence on the fate of Europe becomes quite obvious if one imagines the course events might have taken during one year only, during 1923, if we had had a common frontier with Germany. There are innumerable reasons to think that the German developments would have shaped themselves in an entirely different manner. Nor can one doubt that without our military intervention—and our defeat—the revolutionary movement within Poland would have taken on an incomparably more favorable aspect. As far as I am aware, Lenin himself attached a great importance to the "Warsaw blunder." And yet in his appraisal of Lenin's tactical *élan,* Radek was quite correct. Of course, after we failed to achieve the hoped-for results from our "sounding" of the Polish working masses; after we were thrown back—and this was unavoidable because in the political calm which reigned in Poland our intervention could be nothing more than a guerrilla raid; after we were compelled to sign the Riga Treaty, it was easy to come to the conclusion that the opponents of the March on Warsaw were right, that it would have been better to call a halt in time and render secure our frontier with Germany. Hindsight made all this clear. What was so striking in the whole enterprise was the audacity and courage of Lenin's conception. The risk was extraordinary; but so was the magnitude of the goal. The possible failure did not threaten the very existence of the Soviet state; at the most it might have weakened our country.

We can leave to future historians the task of judging whether it was worth accepting worse conditions at Brest for the sake of exposing them to the full view of the European working masses. It was absolutely clear that once we had exposed them, we had no choice but to sign what was forced upon us. And here Lenin saved the situation by his clear, precise thinking and his resolution.

"And if the Germans maintain their offensive? And if they march on Moscow?"

"Then we shall withdraw farther east, to the Urals, all the

time declaring our readiness to conclude peace. The Kuznetsk Basin is rich in coal. We shall set up an Uralo-Kuznetsk Republic based on the regional industry and the Kuznetsk coal and supported by the proletariat of Ural and by as many workers as we can move with us from Moscow and Petrograd. We shall hold out. If need be, we shall retreat even deeper, beyond the Urals. We may reach Kamchatka, but we shall hold out. The international situation will be changing a dozen times; from the redoubt of our Uralo-Kuznetsk Republic, we shall spread out again and we shall return to Moscow and Petersburg. But if now we senselessly involve ourselves in a revolutionary war, if we let the elite of our working class and our party perish, then, of course, we shall return nowhere."

At that time the Uralo-Kuznetsk Republic formed an important part of Lenin's arguments. His opponents were often disconcerted when he threw at them the question: "And do you realize that our coalfields in the Kuznetsk Basin are enormous? Together with the Ural iron ore and the Siberian grain we have here a new base." Not always knowing where precisely the Kuznetsk Basin was situated nor what the possible relationship between its coal and Bolshevism and the revolutionary war was, Lenin's interlocutor would either gaze with wide-open eyes or burst out laughing, not quite sure whether Lenin was joking or playing a trick on him. But, as a matter of fact, Lenin was by no means joking; true to himself, he was analyzing the situation through to its very end, to its worst possibilities. To him the concept of the Uralo-Kuznetsk Republic was absolutely necessary in order to strengthen his own —and other peoples'—conviction that all was not lost and that there was no room, that there could be no room, for the strategy of despair.

Fortunately, we never were reduced to the Uralo-Kuznetsk Republic. Nevertheless one can assert that the Uralo-Kuznetsk Republic, which had never materialized, saved the Union of Russian Soviet Federal Socialist Republics.

In any case, to understand and appreciate Lenin's tactics during the Brest Litovsk period, one has to view them together with his policy during October. To have taken a stand against the October uprising and for the Brest Litovsk peace was, in fact, to express in both instances nothing less than a mood of capitulation. The essence of the matter is that Lenin approached the Brest Litovsk capitulation with the same inexhaustible revolutionary energy which secured the party's victory in October. Precisely this intrinsic and as if organic combination of October and Brest Litovsk, of the gigantic sweep with intrepidity and circumspection, of both boldness and foresight, gives a measure of Lenin's method and of his power.

4. The Dispersal of the Constituent Assembly

Lenin raised the question of the Constituent Assembly a few days, or even a few hours, after the insurrection.

"It has to be adjourned," he declared, "and the elections have to be postponed. We must widen the electoral laws so that eighteen-year-olds have the right to vote. We must have time to revise the lists of candidates. Even our own lists are not worth much: They contain a large number of men from the intelligentsia, whose names appear almost accidentally. What we need are workers and peasants. The Kornilovists, the Cadets, should be outlawed."

Some protested: "It is awkward to postpone now. People will see in this an attempt to liquidate the Assembly, especially as we ourselves have accused the Provisional Government of tampering with it."

"Nonsense!" objected Lenin. "Deeds are important, not words. In relation to the Provisional Government the Constituent Assembly represented, or might have represented, progress; in relation to the regime of the Soviets, and with the existing electoral lists, it will inevitably mean retrogression. Why is it inconvenient to postpone it? Will it be convenient if the Constituent Assembly turns out to be composed of a Cadet-Menshevik–Social Revolutionary alliance?"

"By that time we shall be stronger," remonstrated other comrades. "We are still too weak now. The provinces hardly know anything about the Soviet regime, and if the news spreads that we have adjourned the Assembly, we shall be weakened even further."

Sverdlov, who more than others was connected with the provinces, protested vehemently against the adjournment.

Lenin stood alone. He kept on shaking his head, dissatisfied, and went on repeating, "You are wrong; it's clearly a mistake which can prove very costly. Let us hope that the revolution will not have to pay for it with its life . . ."

Yet when the decision not to postpone the elections was taken, Lenin devoted all his attention to organizational matters connected with the preliminaries to the Assembly. In the meantime it became evident that we would be in a minority, even if the left Social Revolutionaries gave us their support; the fact was that they and their right-wingers had a common slate and were tricked all around.

"Of course, the Constituent Assembly should be dissolved," Lenin kept on saying, "but what is to be done with the left Social Revolutionaries?"

Old Natanson gave us a great deal of encouragement. He came to "consult" us, and right from the beginning said, "Well, I think that nevertheless the Assembly will have to be scattered by force."

"Bravo!" exclaimed Lenin, "That's right, that's right! But will your people agree to this?"

"Some are hesitant, but I believe that in the end they will agree," answered Natanson.

This was the heyday of the left Social Revolutionaries' extreme radicalism; they did indeed agree to the dispersal of the Constituent Assembly.

"And suppose we unite our faction in the Constituent Assembly and your faction with the Central Executive Committee and in this way form a convention?" proposed Natanson.

"What for?" asked Lenin, visibly annoyed. "To imitate the French Revolution? The dispersal of the Constituent will consolidate the Soviet system. Your plan will muddle everything up; we shall have neither fish nor flesh . . ."

Natanson tried to prove that by acting according to his plan we would be able to take some of the Assembly's authority onto our shoulders; but soon he was persuaded to give up his idea.

Lenin undertook to deal with the problem of the Assembly there and then.

"The mistake is obvious," he argued. "We have gained power and at the same time we have put ourselves into a position in which we are compelled to use military means in order to win it anew."

He was preparing the action against the Assembly extremely carefully, giving a great deal of thought to every detail and subjecting Uritsky, who, to his distress, had been appointed the Commissar for the Constituent Assembly, to intense interrogation. Among other measures, he also demanded that one of the Latvian regiments, consisting almost entirely of workers, be posted to Petrograd.

"If it comes to anything, the *muzhik* may falter," he said, "and here we need proletarian determination."

The Bolshevik delegates to the Constituent Assembly, who began arriving from all corners of Russia, were, under Lenin's pressure and Sverdlov's directions, assigned to various factories, workshops, and military centers. They constituted an impor-

tant element in the organization of the "supplementary revolution" of January 5. The Social Revolutionary deputies
considered it incompatible with the high calling of a representative of the nation to take part in any struggle. "The people have elected us—let the people defend us." In truth, these
provincial *petit bourgeois* just did not know what to do with
themselves, and the majority were simply frightened. But they
prepared thoroughly for the whole ceremonial of the first session; they brought candles with them just in case the Bolsheviks cut off the electricity supply, and a large reserve of sandwiches just in case the Bolsheviks deprived them of food. That
was how democracy marched into battle against dictatorship
—fully armed with candles and sandwiches. The people, however, did not even give a thought to defending those who considered themselves the nation's representatives, but were, in
fact, only faint shadows of an outworn period of the revolution.

During the liquidation of the Constituent Assembly I was
in Brest Litovsk. When, soon afterward, I returned to Petrograd for some consultation, Lenin commented, "Of course,
we took great risks in not adjourning the convocation of the
Assembly; of course, we acted very, very imprudently. But in
the end it turned out all to the good. By dispersing the Constituent Assembly, the Soviet regime, in the name of proletarian dictatorship, openly and finally put an end to formal democracy.
This lesson will not be forgotten." That was how theoretical generalization went hand in hand with the practical use of
Latvian infantry regiments. It must have been at that time that
Lenin was definitely reaching the conclusions which later,
during the First Congress of the Comintern, he so brilliantly
formulated in his theses on democracy.

The critique of formal democracy has, as we know, its own
long history. The 1848 revolution and its transitory character
was seen by us and by our predecessors as the crumbling of
political democracy which was to be followed by "social" democracy. But bourgeois society knew how to make "social"

democracy take the place which democracy pure and simple could no longer maintain. There was a long period in political history when "social" democracy, nourished by the critique of pure democracy, in fact differed little from the latter; it took over all the latter's tasks and became permeated with all its vices. Not once has it happened in the past that the opposition was called upon to solve, by conservative means, those problems which the compromised regime of yesterday was unable to solve. From a transitory stage, which was to serve only as a preparatory period for proletarian dictatorship, democracy became the highest criterion, the supreme tribunal, the sacred temple, in essence the acme of hypocrisy, of bourgeois society. This was what happened in Russia. Having received a mortal blow in October, the bourgeoisie still tried in January to re-incarnate itself in the phantomlike, holy, Constituent Assembly. The victorious developments of the proletarian revolution which followed the open, frank, and brutal dispersal of the Constituent Assembly, gave formal democracy the *coup de grâce* from which it was never to recover. This was why Lenin was right when he remarked, "In the end it all turned out to the good!"

In the Assembly of Social Revolutionaries the February republic had an opportunity to die its second death.

Against the background of the general impressions connected with the official "February" Russia and with the Petrograd Soviet, composed then of Menshevik and Social Revolutionaries, one figure of an SR delegate stands out clearly, as if it were only yesterday. I have no idea who he was, or where he came from, but he must have arrived from the provinces. Outwardly, he looked like a young schoolteacher from a worthy pedagogical institute: flat-nosed, bespectacled, high-cheekboned, nearly beardless—the face of a simpleton. I saw him at the session during which the socialist ministers presented themselves for the first time before the Soviet. Chernov, diffusely, eloquently, with sickening flourishes, coquetry, and sweet persuasiveness, was explaining why he and the others had joined the government and what would be the blessed consequences of this act. I remember particularly one tiresome phrase which the orator repeated dozens of times: "You have pulled us into the government and it is up to you to pull us out." The schoolmaster gazed at the speaker with eyes full of intense admiration. He had the look and feel of a faithful pilgrim who had reached a famous shrine and is about to hear the wisdom of a holy man. The speech flowed endlessly; the audience now and again grew bored and there was a slight murmur. But the schoolmaster's sources of veneration seemed to be inexhaustible. "This is what our revolution—or rather *their* revolution—looks like," I said to myself during the session of the Soviets of 1917. There was loud applause after Chernov finished his speech. Only in one corner a small group of dissatisfied Bolsheviks exchanged their impressions. They came at once to the fore when they supported, in a friendly fashion, my criticism of the "ministerialism" and the politics of national defense preached by the Mensheviks and the SR's. The reverent schoolmaster was greatly disturbed and frightened. He was not indignant. During those days he dared not be angry with an emigré who had returned to his fatherland. But he could not understand how one could be against such a happy and, in all respects, admirable event such as the entry of Chernov into the Provisional Government. The young man sat a few steps from me, and on his face, which I used as a barometer of the meeting, fear and incomprehension struggled with a faith as yet unshattered. The image remained with me forever—it personified the February revolution, or its better aspect: simple, naïve, mediocre, *petit bourgeois* schoolmasterish; it also had another face, much worse, that of Dan and Chernov.

Not without reason and not by accident, Chernov turned out to be the President of the Constituent Assembly. He was raised up by the February revolution, the still slow-moving, republican revolution of half-Oblomovs,[1] still full of delusions, and oh! how ingenuous in some ways and oh! how artful in others. The drowsy *muzhik,* through such agents as these devout tutors, was raising up and elevating the Chernovs; Chernov himself was receiving the mandate not without a "truly Russian" grace and equally "truly Russian" deceitfulness.[2] What I am trying to say is that Chernov was also in a sense a national type. I am saying that he was *also* a national type because some four years ago I wrote about Lenin's national characteristics. The juxtaposition, or even an indirect pairing of these two figures may seem incongruous; and it would indeed be foolish and incongruous if we were to link the two personalities. But what I have in mind are "elemental" national features and the way they become embodied and reflect themselves. Chernov is the epigone of the old revolutionary tradition of the intelligentsia; Lenin is at one and the same time its crowning achievement and its complete repudiation. In the old intellectual there lived a nobleman, beating his breast and babbling profusely about his debt to the people; among the old intelligentsia you could find the reverential tutor who lived with his aunt surrounded by icons, and who opened a window—just a slit—into the world of critical thought; there might have also been a nice enlightened peasant hesitating between socialization and the chunk of a farm offered by Stolypin;[3] there might also have been a solitary worker who rubbed shoulders a little with the gentlemen-students and, as a result, had left his own people but had not be-

---

[1] *Translator's note:* Oblomov is a character in Goncharov's novel and symbolizes the will-less, indolent, inert Russian nobleman.

[2] *Translator's note:* Trotsky uses the word *rasseiskoi,* which here is an ironical distortion of the word "Russian."

[3] *Translator's note:* Stolypin was the Minister of the Interior, and later the Prime Minister in the period of counterrevolutionary terror after the defeat of the 1905 revolution. In November, 1906, he introduced an "agrarian reform" which proclaimed the right of any peasant who possessed land to separate it from the lands run by the village communes.

come one with the others. All this is represented by "Chernovism" with its honeyed tongue, its formlessness—mediocre through and through. In the days of Sophia Perovskaya[4] there was idealism among the intellectuals, but of this there was hardly a trace in Chernov's world. What had been added had come from the new industrial-commercial Russia and is well-expressed in the maxim of our traders: "Who does not cheat does not sell."

In his time Herzen was an immense and wonderful influence on the development of Russian thought. But let him outstay his epoch by half a century, deprive him of the gorgeous plumage of his talent, turn him into his own epigone, place him against the background of the years 1905–1917 and you have an element of "Chernovism." It is much more difficult to perform a similar operation with Chernyshevsky; but all the Chernovs have in themselves something of a caricature of Chernyshevsky. The connection with Mikhailovsky[5] is more direct because Mikhailovsky himself outlived his ideas. Under the surface of the whole of our development, as under Chernovism, there is the peasant element, refracted in the immature half-educated *petit bourgeois* of small towns and villages or in the overripe and already slightly decaying intelligentsia. The culmination of Chernovism was, of necessity, ephemeral. In February there was a first tremor: the soldier, the worker, and the *muzhik* woke up; gradually the jolt affected the volunteers in the army, the teachers, the students, the lawyers; then it made itself felt in the "contact commissions" and other cleverly devised institutions; that shock lifted the Chernovs to democratic heights, while in the meantime . . . down below, the very foundations had shifted and the

---

[4] *Translator's note:* A young member of the *Narodnaya Volya,* who took part in the attempt on the life of Czar Alexander II. She was sentenced to death and executed in April, 1881.

[5] *Translator's note:* N. K. Mikhailovsky (1842–1904), Russian sociologist and journalist, the ideologue of the liberal Populists, was opposed to Russian Marxism.

democratic peaks were left suspended in the void. That was
why between February and October the whole spirit of Chernovism found its expression in the appeal: "Stay a while—
time—you are so beautiful!" But time did not stand still. The
devil was taking possession of the soldier; the *muzhik* began
balking, even the tutor was quickly shedding the reverence of
February. In consequence the Chernovs, their robes blown
about by the wind, slithered unbecomingly from unimagined
heights into the muddy puddles of reality.

There was a peasant undercurrent in Leninism too, in so
far as it exists in our proletariat and runs through the whole
of our history. Fortunately, our history was not one of apathy
or the spirit of Oblomov alone; there was action too. Our
peasant was full of senseless prejudice, but he was also capable of good sense. All that was action and courage, all that
was hatred of oppression and of stagnation, all the contempt
for weak characters—in a word all those features which determine a mass movement formed by a shift in social classes
and by the dynamics of class struggle, found their expression
in Bolshevism. The peasant element broke open in this case in
the proletariat, that is, in the most dynamic force in our history
and in history at large; and Lenin was the perfect embodiment
of that force. Precisely in this sense the peasant-national element was raised to the highest point by Lenin; while in Chernovs the same national feature remained at its lowest.

The tragicomic episode of January 5, 1919 (the dispersal
of the Constituent Assembly) was in principle the last skirmish between Leninism and Chernovism. "In principle," because in reality there was no skirmish at all, only a small and
pathetic demonstration of the rearguard of "democracy," bow-
ing itself off the stage, armed with its candles and sandwiches.
All the blown-up illusions collapsed like pricked balloons; all
the cheap decorations fell to the ground; all the puffed-up
moral strength was exposed in all its half-witted impotence.
Finis.

5. *The Business of Government*

In Petersburg power is taken. The government has to be formed.

"What shall we call it?" asked Lenin, thinking aloud. "Let us not use the word Minister; it is a dull, hackneyed title."

"Perhaps 'Commissars,' " I suggested, "only there are too many Commissars just now. Perhaps Supreme Commissar? . . . No, 'Supreme' sounds wrong too. What about 'People's Commissar'?"

"People's Commissar? Well, this sounds all right. And the government as a whole?"

"Council of People's Commissars?"

"Council of People's Commissars," echoed Lenin. "That's splendid; it smells of revolution."

This last sentence I remember by heart.[1]

Behind the scenes laborious negotiations went on with *Vikzhel* (Executive Committee of the Railway Workers' Union), with the left SR's, and with others. I have not much to say about all this. I only remember the violent indignation with which Lenin reacted to *Vikzhel*'s insolent demands and his no less violent indignation against those among us who were impressed by these demands. However, we continued the negotiations because for the time being we had to reckon with *Vikzhel*.

On Comrade Kamenev's initiative, Kerensky's decree intro-

[1] T. Miliutin related this episode somewhat differently, but my version seems to me more correct. In any case, Lenin's words, "it smells of revolution," referred to my suggestion of calling the government as a whole the Council of People's Commissars.

ducing capital punishment for troops was repealed. I do not remember now before which body Kamenev brought his proposal, but it must have been the Military Revolutionary Committee, and he must have done it on the morning of October 25 (November 7). I recall that I was present when the proposal was made and that I did not object. Lenin was not there at the time; it must have been before his arrival at the Smolny. When he learned about this first piece of legislation, his anger was unbounded.

"Nonsense," he kept on repeating. "How can one make a revolution without firing squads? Do you think you will be able to deal with all your enemies by laying down your arms? What other means of repression do you have? Imprisonment? No one attaches any importance to this during a civil war when each side hopes to win."

Kamenev tried to prove that the abolished decree was introduced by Kerensky especially against soldier-deserters. But Lenin was adamant. For him it was clear that the abolition of capital punishment resulted from a lack of serious considerations of all the enormous difficulties which we were going to encounter presently.

"It's a mistake," he went on, "an inadmissible weakness, a pacifist illusion," and so on, and so on. He proposed to rescind the decree straightway. There was opposition, and the argument was raised that this would produce a very unfortunate impression. Someone said it would be better simply to have recourse to a firing squad when it becomes obvious that there is no other way. Thus, the matter ended.

From the first day of the upheaval the bourgeois newspapers and those of the Social Democrats and the Mensheviks kept up a unanimous chorus of wolves, jackals, and rabid dogs. Only the *Novoye Vremya* tried to adopt a "loyal" tone, tail between hind legs.

"Aren't we going to bridle this rabble?" Lenin kept asking

at every opportunity. "Well, excuse me, what sort of dictatorship is this?"

The newspapers repeatedly took up the slogan: "Rob what had been robbed" and churned it up on all possible occasions, in their leading articles, in their poems, and in their correspondence columns.

"They do stick to that 'rob what had been robbed,' " said Lenin one day in comic despair.

"Whose words were they?" I asked, "or were they just invented?"

"No, somehow I said it myself," answered Lenin. "I said it and then forgot all about it, and they have made of these words a whole political program." And, discouraged, he waved his hand in jest.

Anyone who knew anything about Lenin was aware that one of his strong points was the ability in every instance to distinguish the essence of the matter from the form. But it might be worthwhile to stress that he also attached importance to the form, realizing how much the formal side of things dominates people's mind; in this way he was able to invest formality with substance. From the moment of the deposition of the Provisional Government, Lenin systematically, in small things as well as in great, acted as a government should. We had not yet any governmental apparatus; our contact with the provinces was nonexistent; we were sabotaged by officialdom; *Vikzhel* was interfering with our telegraphic connections with Moscow; we had no money; we had no army. But all the time and everywhere Lenin ruled by decisions, decrees, and orders in the name of the government. It goes without saying that Lenin less than anybody else was inclined to be impressed by the magic of formality. He was acutely conscious of the fact that our strength lay in this new governmental apparatus which was organizing itself from below, from the Petersburg districts. But in order to conduct the work "from above," from the offices deserted by the saboteurs, in conjunction with the creative work from below, this formal tone was needed, the tone of a government which today is still suspended in a vacuum, but which tomorrow or the day after will become a force, and for this reason already acts as a force. This formality was also needed in order to discipline our own brethren. The governmental apparatus was slowly spreading its net over the turmoil and ferment, over revolutionary improvisations of advanced proletarian groups.

Lenin's office and my own were situated on the two opposite sides of the Smolny Institute. The corridor which connected, or rather separated, the two rooms was so long that Lenin, jokingly, proposed to establish liaison by means of cyclists. We communicated by telephone; often sailors would be coming in, bringing those extraordinary notes from Lenin. Written on small pieces of paper, they contained two or three strongly worded blunt sentences, with most important passages underlined twice or thrice, and with a final question— also set out bluntly. Several times a day I used to march along the unending corridor, resembling a beehive, to Vladimir Ilyich's office for discussions. In the center of our preoccupations were military questions. The running of the Ministry of Foreign Affairs I left entirely to Comrades Markin and Zalkind. I limited myself to producing a few notes of a propagandist character and receiving a small number of visitors.

The German offensive was creating the most difficult problems for us, and we had no means to resolve them; nor did we have any possibility of finding those means or creating them. We started by an appeal. My draft proposal—"Socialist Fatherland in Danger"—was discussed with the left Social Revolutionaries. The SR's, as new converts to internationalism, were bothered by the title of the appeal. Lenin, on the contrary, approved of it. "It shows immediately that we have made a 180-degree turn as far as the question of national defense is concerned. That is just what is needed."

One of the final paragraphs contained a warning that whoever gave help to the enemy would be put to death on the spot. The left Social Revolutionary Steinberg—I do not know what queer wind blew him toward the revolution and into the Council of People's Commissars—protested against this cruel threat which, according to him, spoiled the "dramatic effect of the appeal."

"On the contrary!" exclaimed Lenin. "Exactly in this resides the genuine revolutionary 'dramatic effect.'" (He pronounced the words "dramatic effect" with an ironical twist.) "Do you really think that we shall come out victorious without any revolutionary terror?"

This was during the time when Lenin stressed the inevitability of terror at every suitable opportunity. Any signs of sentimentality, of easygoing cordiality, of softness—and there was a great surplus of all this—angered him not intrinsically, but because he saw in them a sign that even the elite of the working class was not fully aware of all the extraordinarily difficult tasks which could be accomplished only by means of quite extraordinary energy.

"They," he used to say about our enemies, "they run the risk of losing everything. And yet they have hundreds of thousands of men who went through the experience of war, who are well-fed, courageous; they have officers, junkers, the sons of landlords and industrialists, sons of policemen and rich peasants, who are ready for anything. And here are those, excuse the word, 'revolutionaries' who imagine that we shall achieve our revolution in a nice way, with kindness? What have they learned? What do they understand by 'dictatorship'? And what sort of a dictatorship will that be if they themselves are ninnies?"

Admonitions of this kind could be heard dozens of times daily, and they were always aimed at somebody present who was suspected of "pacifism." Lenin would not let an occasion pass—when the talk was about revolution or dictatorship, especially during the meetings of the *Sovnarkom* (Council of People's Commissars) or in the presence of Left SR's or vacillating Communists—without remarking, "Where is our dictatorship? Well, show it to me! We have a mess, not a dictatorship." He liked the word "mess" very much. "If we are incapable of shooting a White Guard saboteur, then what sort of a great revolution is this? Just look what those bourgeois wretches write in their newspapers! Where is the dictatorship? Nothing but prattle and mess. . . ."

These exhortations expressed Lenin's real state of mind, but they also had their well-defined purpose. True to his method, Lenin was hammering in the realization that extremely stern measures would be inevitable for the safety of the revolution.

The impotence of the new governmental apparatus became strikingly evident when the Germans went over to the offensive.

"Yesterday we were still firmly in the saddle," said Lenin when we were alone, "and today we are barely holding on to the mane. That is a lesson for us! That will teach us how to get out of our accursed Oblomovism! That will teach us how to introduce order into our affairs, to get to grips with our work as we should if we don't want to remain slaves. Indeed, this will be a lesson for us but only . . . only if the Germans together with the Whites don't manage to bowl us over!"

Once, all of a sudden, Lenin asked, "And what if the White Guards kill you and me? Will Bukharin and Sverdlov manage on their own?"

"Oh, well . . . they won't kill us," I answered, laughing.

"Devil only knows," said Lenin and also laughed. At that, the conversation ended.

In one of the halls of the same Smolny Institute the General Staff used to hold their meetings. This was the most disorderly of all establishments. One could never understand who commanded, who issued orders and to whom. Here was raised, for the first time in a general manner, the question of military specialists. We had already acquired some experience in this matter during the struggle against Krasnov[2] when we appointed Colonel Muraviev[3] as commander, and he, on his part, entrusted the conduct of the operations at Pulkovo to Colonel Valden. We assigned four sailors and one soldier to Muraviev. They were instructed to watch both men and not to take their hands off their revolvers. Such were the beginnings of the system of army commissars. This experience proved useful to a certain extent when the Supreme Military Council was set up.

"Without serious and experienced military personnel we shall not manage to overcome chaos," I kept telling Vladimir Ilyich after each visit to the General Staff.

"Yes, it seems you are right. But how to guard against treachery?"

"We shall assign a commissar to each."

"Let's assign two," exclaimed Lenin, "and tough ones at that. It is impossible that we should not have tough Communists."

In this way the Supreme Military Council came into existence.

The transfer of government to Moscow caused a great deal of friction. Some said that this would be abandoning Petrograd which laid the foundations of the revolution; the workers would not understand this; the Smolny had become the symbol of the Soviet regime, and now you propose to liquidate it, and so on, and so forth. Lenin was beside himself with anger.

"How can one by such sentimental nonsense obscure the whole problem of the revolution's future? If the Germans in

[2] *Translator's note:* Cossack General Krasnov was a monarchist, who in the last days of October marched with Kerensky on Petersburg.

[3] *Translator's note:* Colonel Muraviev who, after the uprising, sympathized with the left Social Revolutionaries, later tried to go over to the enemy. In 1918 he died either by his own hand or a Bolshevik's bullet.

one big swoop overrun Petersburg—and all of us—then the revolution perishes. If the government is in Moscow, then the fall of Petersburg will be a grievous blow, but only a blow. How is it that you don't see this, that you don't understand? Moreover, if we, in the present conditions, remain in Petersburg we are only increasing the military danger; it is as if we were inviting the Germans to take Petersburg. If the government is in Moscow, the temptation to seize Petersburg is much smaller. What advantage is there in occupying a hungry revolutionary city if this occupation is not decisive for the fate of the revolution and of peace? Why do you prattle about the symbolic importance of the Smolny! The Smolny is what it is because we are in it. When we are in the Kremlin, all your symbolism will move to the Kremlin."

Finally, the opposition to the move was defeated. The government was transferred to Moscow. I remained for some time in Petrograd as president of the Military Revolutionary Committee, if I am not mistaken. When I went to Moscow, I found Vladimir Ilyich in the Kremlin, in the so-called Cavalry Building. The "mess," that is, the chaos and disorder, was just as great here as it had been in the Smolny. Good-humoredly Lenin was scolding the Muscovites who were preoccupied by questions of hierarchy, and gradually, step by step, he was tightening the reins.

The government, which in its composition was changing quite often, developed the feverish activity of passing ever new decrees. Every session of the Council of People's Commissars in this period presented a picture of legislative improvisation on a grand scale. Everything was in its beginnings, everything had to be built anew. There was no use looking for "precedents," because history had not supplied any. There was not even enough time to make simple inquiries. The issues debated were only those which from the revolutionary point of view were most urgent—this contributed to chaos and disorder. Great problems were often mixed up with small ones in a most fantastic manner. Secondary practical issues led to the most complicated questions of principle. Decrees did not always accord with one another, far from it. And Lenin more than once, even publicly, made ironic remarks about the lack of consistency found in our creativity in the field of decrees. But in the end, all these contradictions, even those which seemed very sharp when considered from the point of view of the practical tasks of the moment, were permeated by revolutionary thought trying to chart new roads leading to a new order of human relationships.

It goes without saying that the leadership in all this activity was Lenin's. Untiringly, he presided, for five or six hours at a stretch, over the meetings of the Council of People's Commissars, which at that period took place every day; he directed the debates passing from subject to subject, severely limiting speakers' time according to his pocket watch which soon was replaced by a chairman's chronometer. As a rule, the topics of discussion were put on the agenda without any previous preparation, and, as I said before, always demanding extreme urgency. Very often neither the chairman nor the Commissars were familiar with the essentials of a problem until it became the subject of the debate. But the discussion was always concise. For the preliminary exposition of the theme the speaker had no more than five or ten minutes, and yet the chairman somewhat gropingly always found the right line along which to steer the debate. When there was a meeting at which many people were present, among them specialists or people unknown to Lenin, he resorted to his favorite gesture. He would put his right hand over his forehead and eyes and look between his stretched fingers. Thus, playing peek-a-boo, he observed the speaker and the participants very intently and attentively and saw exactly what he needed to see. On narrow strips of paper, in small writing (economy measures!) he noted the names of the speakers. He kept one eye on the watch which now and again appeared over the table to remind the orator that his time was up. Meanwhile, he quickly jotted down the essential conclusions resulting from the debate. In addition, in order to save time, he was sending out to some participants short notes in which he asked for particular information.

These notes would have constituted a rich and important epistolary documentation of the technique of Soviet legislation. Most of them, unfortunately, were lost, if only because the answer was usually written on the reverse side of the paper, and on receiving it, the chairman straightway crumpled it up or tore it to bits. Then at a certain moment Lenin would read the salient points of the resolution, always expressed in a dry style and with didactic lucidity, so that all points would be clearly stressed and unlikely to lead to confusion. After that the discussion either was brought to an end or evolved to some practical issues or to some supplementary elucidation. Lenin's "points" formed the basis of a decree. To conduct this kind of work, one needed, apart from other qualities, an immensely creative imagination.

The word "imagination" may, at first glance, seem inappropriate in this context, and yet it expresses the very essence of the thing. There are various aspects of imagination: An engineer-designer needs imagination just as much as a bohemian romantic. One of the most valuable attributes of imagination is its ability to conceive of people, things, and phenomena as they really are, although one might never have had a chance to observe them. The ability to make use of one's experience and theoretical principles, to coordinate disparate hints and pieces of information which are in the air, and to assimilate them, to supplement them, to unite them together according to some unformulated laws of harmony, and, in this way, to reconstitute in all its concrete reality a field of human existence—this is the kind of imagination so indispensable to any legislator, administrator, or leader, especially in a revolutionary epoch. Lenin's strength lay, in great measure, in the richness of his realistic imagination. The tense and concentrated manner in which he pursued his aim always had in it this element of concreteness, of reality; otherwise it would never have been so purposeful.

Lenin himself, in the *Iskra*, I think, expressed for the first time the idea that in the complex chain of political acts one had to be able, at a given moment, to discern the main, the central, link in order to seize it and to impart to the whole chain the desired direction. More than once Lenin used to return to this conception and even to the metaphor. From his conscious mind this methodological notion seemed to have permeated into his subconscious and in the end it became his second nature. During the most critical periods, when he was faced with tactical decisions involving a high degree of risk or exceptional responsibility, Lenin was able to set aside all that was irrelevant, all that was secondary, all that was inessential and could be deferred. This does not mean that he considered only the main, the central part of his task, ignoring the details. On the contrary, he viewed the problem with which he had to come to grips in all its concrete reality, approaching it from every side, weighing all its details, sometimes even tertiary ones, searching for ever new points of attack, trying to find new ways of exercising pressure, of checking facts, and calling for action. But in all this he would never lose sight of "the link" which at that particular moment he thought was of decisive importance. He brushed aside not only everything directly or indirectly in conflict with the job in hand, but also everything which might disperse attention or slacken tension. In the most critical moments he became as if deaf and blind to all that went beyond the cardinal problem which absorbed him. In the mere posing of other questions, "neutral ones," he saw a danger from which he instinctively recoiled. Later on, when the critical hurdle was happily cleared, Lenin would now and again exclaim, "And yet we quite forgot to do this or that," or "We missed an opportunity because we were so preoccupied by the main thing." Someone would answer him: "But this question had been posed, and this proposal had been made, only you did not want to hear anything!"

"Didn't I? Impossible!" he would say, "and I don't remember a thing."

At that point he would burst out laughing, with malicious laughter in which there was an admission of "guilt"; and he would make a characteristic gesture of raising his arm and moving it helplessly down, as if resigned: "Well, one cannot do everything." This "shortcoming" of his was only the obverse side of his talent to mobilize to the utmost degree all his inner forces. Precisely this talent made of him the greatest revolutionary in history.

In his theses on peace, written at the beginning of January, 1918, Lenin says that "for its success socialism in Russia needs a certain spell of time, *at least a few months.*" These words seem absolutely incomprehensible now. Wasn't this a slip of the pen? Did he not mean "a few years" or "a few decades"? No, this was no slip. One could probably find quite a number of statements of this kind. I very well remember how, in the first period, in the Smolny, Lenin at the session of the Sovnarkom repeatedly said that in half a year we would have socialism and would become one of the most powerful states. Not only the left Social Revolutionaries used to raise their eyebrows questioningly and, in surprise, glance at one another, but keep silent. This was Lenin's "method of persuasion." This was his way of teaching people around him to consider all problems from the viewpoint of socialist construction—not in the long perspective of the "final aim," but in the immediate perspective of today and tomorrow. And here, in this sudden transition, he had recourse to a mode peculiarly his own—a certain exaggeration: Yesterday we maintained that socialism is the "final aim," today we have to think, talk, and act in such a manner as to secure the socialist order in a few months. Was this then a didactic trick only? No, not just a trick. There was something more to Lenin's pedagogical firmness; there was the force of his idealism and the tenacity of his indomitable will which at the sharp turns of history made him cut corners and foreshorten distances. *He believed in what he was saying.* And so the fantastic date for socialism —six months hence—testified also to the same Leninist spirit which showed itself in his realistic approach to every immediate task. The deep and unyielding conviction that there were tremendous possibilities for human development for which one could, one should, pay the price of suffering and sacrifice— this was the hallmark of Leninism.

In the most difficult circumstances, in the course of the most wearing daily tasks, amid shortages of food and all other disasters, in the heat of the civil war, Lenin assiduously worked on the elaboration of the Soviet Constitution, endeavoring scrupulously to achieve a balance between the secondary and tertiary needs of the state apparatus and the fundamental tasks of the proletarian dictatorship in a peasant country.

The Constitutional Commission decided, for some reasons, to revise Lenin's "Declaration of the Rights of the Toilers" so that it should "accord" somehow with the Constitution. When I returned from the front to Moscow, I received the text of this revised "Declaration," or, in any case, a part of it. I was looking through all these materials in Lenin's office, in his and Sverdlov's presence. We were in the process of preparing the Fifth Congress of the Soviets.

"Why, in fact, should the 'Declaration' be revised?" I asked Sverdlov who directed the work of the Constitutional Commission.

Vladimir Ilyich, interested, raised his head.

"Well, the Commission found that between the text of the

Declaration and the text of the Constitution there are discrep-
ancies and also inexact formulations," answered Yakov Mi-
khailovich.

"In my view the Commission was wrong," I said. "The
Declaration was adopted and became a historical document—
what is the sense in revising it?"

"Quite right," interjected Vladimir Ilyich. "In my opinion
all this was quite useless. Let this nursling live, untidy and
unkempt as it is; still, it is the child of the revolution . . .
Will it be any better after a visit to the hairdresser?"

Sverdlov out of a sense of duty at first tried to defend the
action of the Commission, but soon he agreed with us. I understood that Vladimir Ilyich, who more than once had to
oppose this or that proposal of the Constitutional Commission, did not want to take up the struggle on the wording of
the "Declaration" of which he was the author. He was, nevertheless, extremely pleased that he found the support of a
"third party" turning up unexpectedly and in the nick of time.
We agreed, all three of us, not to revise the Declaration, and
the wonderful baby was spared the solicitude of a hairdresser . . .

The study of Soviet legislation and its evolution, with particular attention to the main turning points connected with
the course of the revolution itself, and with the class relationship of society, is an immensely important task, because conclusions drawn from it may be, and should be, of great practical significance.

The collection of Soviet decrees forms in a certain sense a
part, and not a negligible part, of the complete works of
Vladimir Ilyich Lenin.

6. The Czechoslovaks and the Left Social Revolutionaries

The spring of 1918 was very hard indeed. Sometimes one had the feeling that everything was slipping away, going to pieces, that there was nothing to hold on to, nothing to lean on. On the one hand it was quite obvious that had it not been for the October upheaval, the country would have fallen into decay. On the other, in the spring of 1918 one had to pose the question: Will this country, so exhausted, so ruined, and so desperate, have enough vitality to support the new regime? There were no supplies. There was no army. The governmental machinery was just beginning to be organized. Plots and conspiracies were spreading like festering sores. The Czechoslovak Army on our soil behaved like an independent power; we could do nothing, or nearly nothing, to oppose it.

Once, in those terrible days of 1918, Vladimir Ilyich said to me, "Today I received a delegation of workers.[1] I talked to them and then one man said, 'We can see that you, Comrade Lenin, are also taking the side of the capitalists.' You know, it was the first time that I heard such words. And I must admit, I was so taken aback that I did not know what to answer. If this was not just a wicked man and not a Menshevik, then here is an alarming symptom."

Relating this episode to me Lenin seemed to be more depressed and shaken than he was when, later on, bad news was coming from the front about the fall of Kazan or about a direct military threat to Petersburg. This was understandable: Kazan

[1] I very much regret that I cannot remember what the business of that delegation was.

and even Petersburg could be lost and then regained, but the trust of the workers constitutes the real, the fundamental capital of the party.

"I have the impression," I told Vladimir Ilyich then, "that the country, like a patient emerging from grave illnesses, is now in need of solid nourishment, of peace, of attention and care, in order to survive and recover; a slight shock may be fatal."

"Yes, this is my impression too," agreed Lenin. "Such frightening anemia! Now any concussion is dangerous."

And just then the whole business of the Czechoslovak troops threatened to produce the dangerous shock. This foreign army, like a tumor, spread into the limp flesh of southeastern Russia, meeting no resistance, and growing bigger with the accretion of the Social Revolutionaries and other activists of an even whiter hue. Although power was already in Bolshevik hands everywhere, there was still considerable disarray in the provinces. No wonder. It was only in Petersburg and in Moscow that the revolution had been really carried through; in the majority of the provincial cities the October Revolution, like the February one, was carried over the telegraph poles. Here in some places they were linked, in others they were not, just because things were happening in the capital. The formlessness of the social environment, the lack of resistance on the part of the former masters, found its reflection in a certain formlessness on the revolutionary side. The appearance on the scene of the Czechoslovak battalions modified the situation, first to our disadvantage but in the end in our favor. The Whites found a military center around which to rally. But in return the Reds began in all seriousness to rally their own revolutionary forces as well. One could say that it was only with the arrival of the Czechoslovak troops that the people of the Volga region made their October Revolution. But it was not to be accomplished in a day.

On July 3 Vladimir Ilyich phoned me at the Commissariat of War.

"Do you know what has happened?" he said in that muffled voice which with him usually was a sign of some agitation.

"No, what is it?"

"The left SR's threw a bomb at Mirbach; apparently he is gravely wounded. Come straight to the Kremlin; we have to discuss the matter."

A few minutes later I was in Lenin's office. He told me exactly what had happened, and at the same time kept asking over the phone for more details.

"What an affair!" I exclaimed, trying to digest this far from ordinary piece of news. "We cannot complain that life is dull."

"Yes, yes," answered Lenin, laughing nervously. "That's it —the monstrous convulsion of a *petit bourgeois* . . ."

There was irony in his voice when he said *convulsion*. Engels described the same phenomenon as *der rabiat gewordene Kleinbürger*[2]—"the *petit bourgeois* gone berserk."

There followed hurried telephone conversations—brief questions, brief answers—with the Commissariat of Foreign Affairs, with the Department of Home Security (*Cheka*), and other offices. Lenin's thought, as always in critical moments, ran on two planes simultaneously. The Marxist was enriching his historical experience by observing with interest the new frenzy—"the convulsions"—of *petit bourgeois* radicalism; and the leader of the revolution, tirelessly gathering in his hands all the threads of the affair, was deciding what the next practical steps should be. There were rumors of mutiny among the troops of the Home Security Department.

"Well, well, I hope the left SR's will not turn out to be the banana skin on which we shall be destined to slip . . ."

"I just had the very same idea," answered Lenin. "Wouldn't this be precisely the role of the vacillating *petit bourgeois*: to

[2] *Translator's note:* In German in the text.

serve as the banana skin which the White Guards so much wish to throw under our feet? . . . Now we must at any price exercise our influence on the manner in which the Germans will inform Berlin about what has happened. There is more than enough reason for military intervention, especially if one takes into account the fact that Mirbach, no doubt, must have been reporting all the time that we are weak and that the slightest shock would hurt us badly . . ."

Soon Sverdlov arrived—he was the same as always.

"Oh, well," he said, greeting me with a smile, "it looks as if we had to change the Council of People's Commissars into a Military Revolutionary Committee once more."

Lenin still continued to collect information. At that moment, or perhaps a little later, the news of Mirbach's death came. Now we had to go to the embassy to pay our "condolences." It was decided that Lenin should go with Sverdlov and Chicherin, I think. The question arose whether I should also accompany them. After a brief exchange of views, they exempted me from that chore.

"How does one express 'condolences'?" asked Vladimir Ilyich, shaking his head. "I have already talked to Radek about this. I wanted to say *Mitleid,* but apparently one has to say *Beileid.*" With a little chuckle he put on his coat and said firmly to Sverdlov, "Let's go." His expression changed. Now he had a grayish stony look. To drive to the Hohenzollern embassy with expressions of sympathy because of Count Mirbach's death was not an easy thing for Vladimir Ilyich to do. Emotionally, it must have been one of the hardest moments in his life.

It is in such situations that one can judge people. Sverdlov was really incomparable: self-confident, resolute, and resourceful: the best type of Bolshevik. Lenin got to know and appreciate Sverdlov fully precisely during these difficult months. More than once it would happen that Lenin would phone Sverdlov in order to suggest some urgent course of action only to receive the answer, "It has already been done." We often joked about this, saying: "Surely, with Sverdlov it is *already!*"

"Think only, at the beginning we were opposed to his entering the Central Committee," Lenin recalled. "To what an extent we underestimated this man."

Sverdlov was indeed the subject of many discussions, but our view of him was corrected "from below"—by the Congress—and the Congress proved right.[3]

With the revolt of the left Social Revolutionaries we lost a political ally; but in the last analysis this fact only strengthened our position. The party became more united. In many organizations and in the army the importance of Communist cells became better understood. The government's line became firmer. Undoubtedly, the Czechoslovak uprising had a similar effect. It shook the party out of its depression, so widespread since the Brest Litovsk peace. This was the period of mobilization of party members for the Eastern Front. The first contingent, which still contained the left Social Revolutionaries, had already been sent out by Lenin and myself. There, in a rather vague form, were the beginnings of the future organization of political sections. However, news from the Volga region continued to be bad. The treachery of Muraviev and the mutiny of the left Social Revolutionaries caused confusion on the Eastern Front. At once the danger became grave. It was then that a radical change took place.

"Everybody and everything must be mobilized and sent to

[3] Sverdlov is generally regarded as the *first* President of the Central Executive Committee after October. This is not correct. The first President was Kamenev, though he had held this post for a short time only. Sverdlov replaced him on Lenin's initiative when, in connection with some attempts at achieving an alliance with the socialist parties, the inner party struggle became sharper. In the notes attached to Volume XIV of Lenin's *Works* it is alleged that the replacement of Kamenev by Sverdlov was caused by Kamenev's departure for Brest Litovsk. This is not true. As I said above, the change came as a result of the sharpening of inner-party controversy. I remember this all the more clearly because I myself was instructed by the Central Committee, at the meeting of the Executive Committee, to put forward Sverdlov's candidature for the post of President.

the front," said Lenin. "Take off from the 'curtain' all regiments halfway fit to fight and direct them to the Volga districts."

I should perhaps explain that we used to call the "curtain" the thin cordon of troops stationed in the West and facing the territories under German occupation.

"But what about the Germans?"

"The Germans will not budge," answered Lenin. "They won't bother, because it is also in their interest that we should finish with the Czechoslovaks."

This plan was accepted. The regiments sent to the Volga became the nucleus of the future Fifth Army. At the same time it was decided that I should also proceed to the East. I began to organize my military train which was not an easy task then. Vladimir Ilyich too became preoccupied with all the details of this matter; he was sending little notes to me and kept on telephoning.

"Do you have a solid car? Take one from the Kremlin garage."

Then half an hour later: "Are you taking a plane? You should have a plane, it might come in handy."

"There would be planes attached to the army. If it becomes necessary, I may use one," I answered.

Then half an hour later: "My opinion is, however, that you should have a plane on your train. One never knows what might happen," and so on, and on.

Our regiments and divisions, hastily assembled from what remained of the old dispersed army, were, as it is known, lamentably scattered at the first encounter with the Czechoslovak troops.

"In order to overcome this alarming lack of stability we need a strong defense cordon formed by Communists and shock troops," I said to Lenin before my departure. "We must *force* people to fight. If we wait until the *muzhik* is fully awake and becomes alert, it may be too late."

"Of course, you are right," he would answer, "but I fear that even the defense cordon may not react with the required strength. The Russian is tenderhearted and incapable of adopting resolute measures of revolutionary terror. And yet we shall have to try."

It was in Sviazhsk that I learned about the attempt on Lenin's life and about the assassination of Uritsky.[4] These were the tragic days of the revolution's internal crisis. The revolution was doing away with its "tender heart." The sword of the party was becoming at last steeled. Determination was hardening and when necessary even ruthlessness was not lacking. At the front, the political sections together with the detachments of defense and the tribunals were turning the flabby flesh of the young army into muscles and sinew. Soon the change became evident. We retook Kazan and Simbirsk. In Kazan I received from Lenin, who was recovering from his wound, a telegram congratulating us on our first victories in the Volga region.

When soon afterward I came to Moscow for a short visit, together with Sverdlov we went to see Vladimir Ilyich in Gorki. He was recovering quickly, but had not yet returned to work in the capital. We found him in excellent spirits. He wanted to know all the details about the organization of the army, about the morale of the troops, about the activity of the Communists, about the improvement in discipline. He kept on exclaiming, "That's good! That's splendid! The consolidation of the army will soon have its effect on the whole country—everywhere discipline will improve and with it the sense of responsibility."

And indeed at the beginning of autumn one noticed the great change. Of that bloodless debility so evident in the spring

[4] *Translator's note:* M. S. Uritsky, member of Trotsky's Inter-Borough Organization, joined the Bolsheviks in 1917; in 1918 he was assassinated by a young Jewish student named Leonid Kannegiesser as an act of vengeance for the executions of members of his family by the Petrograd Cheki. He was a member of "the Union of Liberation."

there was no longer any trace. Something had moved, had put on strength; and it was remarkable that this time not respite, but, on the contrary, new acute danger saved the revolution by bringing to the surface all the hidden resources of the proletariat's revolutionary energy. When we were getting into the car, Lenin stood gay and cheerful on the balcony. I had seen him so cheerful only on October 25, when in the Smolny he learned about the first military victories of the uprising.

Politically, we finished off the left Social Revolutionaries. We proceeded with the mopping-up operations on the Volga. Lenin recovered from his wound. The revolution grew in power and vigor.

7. Lenin on the Rostrum

Since the October Revolution Lenin has been photographed more than once; he has also been filmed; his voice has been recorded; his speeches taken down in shorthand and printed. Thus we have all the elements of his personality, but only the elements, while the living personality itself consists in their unique and always dynamic combination.

When I try to recall to my mind, to view once again with a fresh eye and to hear with a fresh ear, the first occasion on which I saw and heard Lenin on the platform, I see in front of me a solidly built man, a sturdy, supple figure of medium height; I hear an even-flowing smooth voice with slightly rolling r's, speaking fast, almost without pauses and, at the beginning, without any particular intonation.

His first sentences were usually about generalities: the speaker probing his audience; the proper balance not yet achieved, his gesture uncertain, his gaze seemingly turned inward; the face rather sullen and even morose—his thought working out the way to approach the audience. This introductory period takes more or less time depending on the kind of audience, the subject matter, and the mood of the speaker. Then he finds his right tone. The outlines of the theme become clear. The speaker bends the upper part of the body, sticks his thumbs into the armholes of his waistcoat. These gestures at once swing out head and elbows. The head by itself does not seem exceedingly large on the sturdy and strong body, well built and balanced. What seems enormous is the forehead and the visibly protruding lumps on the skull. He moves his arms about—neither nervously nor in an exaggerated manner. His hand is broad, with short fingers, "plebeian," strong. Like the whole figure, it displays benevolence and kindliness coupled with strength. All this becomes noticeable when the speaker has had the time to warm up. This comes as soon as he sees through his opponents' craftiness or when he himself manages to lead them into a trap. Then, from under the powerful brow Lenin's eyes shine—something of this expression is conveyed by an excellent photograph taken in 1919.

Even the least interested listener, catching that look, pricks his ears up and waits for what is to follow. The high cheekbones glow and seem softened by indulgence and sagacity, behind which one can gauge a keen understanding of men, and of social relations, of circumstances, an understanding which reaches to the very depths of things. The lower part of the face, with the reddish-grayish beard, remains somewhat in the shade. The voice becomes softer, mellower, and at times slyly persuasive.

Then the speaker deals with the supposed objections of his opponent or quotes a malicious sentence from the enemy's writings. Even before he analyzes the hostile idea, he gives you to understand that it is without foundation, superficial, wrong. He pulls his thumbs out of his waistcoat, throws his body gently backwards, takes a few short steps back as if clearing the space for an assault, shrugs his thick-set shoulders either with irony or with despair, and stretches his arms expressively, spreading his palms and fingers.

Condemnation, or derision, or humiliation of the opponent —according to who he is and what his case may be—always comes before the refutation of his idea. The listener is given some notice of what to expect and for what to prepare himself mentally. Then begins the logical offensive. The left hand moves again toward the armhole of the waistcoat, or, even more often, into the trouser-pocket. The right hand follows the path and the rhythm of the argument; the left comes to its assistance when needed. The speaker leans toward the audience, moves to the edge of the platform, bends forward and with a circular motion of his hands, works over his own verbal material. This signifies that we have reached the heart of the matter, the central point of the whole speech.

If there are opponents in the hall, from time to time hostile and critical remarks can be heard. In nine cases out of ten heckling remains unanswered. The speaker says what he has to say, to people to whom he wishes to say it and in a manner which he thinks proper. He does not like to deviate from his trend of thought for the sake of casual repartee. Quick rejoinders are incompatible with his mental concentration. After hostile interruptions his voice becomes harsher, his argument even more strongly focused and more condensed, his thought sharper and his gestures more abrupt. He pays attention to the interruption of an opponent only when it in some way follows his own trend of thought and may help to reach his conclusion more quickly. In such cases his retorts are sometimes quite unexpected because of their deadly simplicity. He lays bare a situation when all his opponents believe he is going to conceal it. Such was more than once the experience of the Mensheviks in the first period of the revolution when they accused Bolshevism of violating democracy and when these accusations still had some freshness.

"Our newspapers have been closed down!"

"Of course, unfortunately not yet all of them. We shall close them all down. [Stormy applause] The proletarian dictatorship will destroy the very roots of the disgraceful commerce in bourgeois opium." [Stormy applause]

The speaker stands erect, his hands in his trouser-pockets. There is no trace of posturing, not a tinge of rhetorical inflections in his voice, but in the whole figure, in the position of the head, in the tight lips, the high cheekbones, the slightly hoarse voice there is unshaken confidence in the correctness of his acts and the justice of his cause. "If you want to fight, then let us fight properly!"

When the speaker attacks not the enemy but his own people, his tone of voice and his gestures are different. In such a case the most violent attack still appeals to "reason." Sometimes the voice of the speaker breaks on a high note; this happens when he crossly denounces some of his own comrades, to shame them, to show that they have understood absolutely nothing, that they are incapable of producing the slightest argument against him, or that there is not the smallest basis for their objections. Just when he says "the slightest" or "the smallest," his voice breaks into a falsetto, and then the most furious tirade acquires an unexpected shade of benevolence.

The speaker has worked out his idea to the end, to the last practical conclusion: his idea—yes, but not its exposition, not the form, except perhaps for a few telling, most pithy, terse, and colorful expressions, which enter the political life of the party and the country and become jingling currency, accepted everywhere. The construction of his sentences is generally top-heavy, with one proposition loaded on another or leading to another. Such a style of speaking presents stenographers—and editors too—with a hard task. But a line of intense and powerful thought cuts its way surely and clearly through these cumbrous phrases.

Is the speaker really a profoundly educated Marxist, thoroughly versed in economic theory, a man of enormous erudition? It seems, now and again, rather that here is a self-educated man who has arrived at an extraordinary degree of understanding all by himself, by the effort of his own brain, without any scientific apparatus, any scientific terminology, and now expounds it all in his own manner. How is it that we get such an impression? Because the speaker has thought out things not only for himself, but also for the broad masses; because his own ideas have been filtered through the experiences of these masses and in the process have become free of theoretical ballast. He can now construct his own exposition of problems without the scientific scaffolding which served him so well when he approached them first himself.

Sometimes, however, the speaker runs up the stairs of his thought too quickly, taking two or three steps at a bound; this happens when the conclusion seems to him too obvious, too plain, and he wants to arrive at it without any further delay.

But, suddenly, he feels that the listeners don't follow him, that the link between him and the audience has snapped. Then he pulls himself together, leaps down, and starts his ascent again, but this time more deliberately, in more measured steps. Even his voice changes: It sheds its excessive tenseness and acquires a compellingly persuasive tone. This "backward leap" of course upsets the whole construction of the discourse. But does one deliver a discourse for the pleasure taken in its construction? Is there any logic more valuable in a political speech than that of a call to action?

When the speaker once more approaches his conclusions, but this time carrying his audience with him without losing anybody on the way, one detects in the hall something like a physical sensation of that well-being and joy which come with a harmonious development of collective thought. Now it only remains to nail the conclusion twice or thrice, so that it holds well, to give it simple, but telling and colorful expression so that it engraves itself on the memory, and then one can afford to give oneself and the listeners a breathing space, to joke and to laugh; in the meantime the collective mind will all the better absorb the newly acquired conclusion.

Lenin's oratorical humor is as plain as all his other artifices, if one can so describe them. In his speeches there are no self-satisfying witticisms, no clever play upon words. His jokes are plain and pithy, intelligible to the masses—they are truly popular. If the political situation gives rise to no anxiety, if the audience consists mostly of "our own people," the speaker is not averse to occasional jocularity. The audience gratefully receives a naïve and simple jest or a jovially malicious characterization, feeling that it is there not just for the fun of it, but that it has some meaning and purpose and serves the same goal.

When the speaker makes a joke, the lower part of his face becames more clearly visible, especially his mouth, with its contagious laughter. The lines of his forehead and skull become softer, the eyes, less piercing, beam cheerfully, the rolling *r*'s become more pronounced; the tension of the concentrated thought relaxes into good-humored happy laughter.

Lenin's speeches are characterized by what is so essential in all his activity: his intentness on the goal, his purposefulness. The speaker is not out to deliver an oration, but to guide toward a conclusion which is to be followed by action. He has different ways of approaching his audience. He explains; he convinces; he shames it; he jokes with it; and then again tries to convince it and again expounds his idea.

What makes for the unity of his speech is not a preconceived formal plan, but a practical aim, clearly defined and valid for that particular moment, which the audience must take in and absorb into its consciousness. Even the humor has to serve that purpose. The jests themselves are utilitarian. A racy word has its practical significance. It has to stir some and curb others. This is why so many of the expressions coined by Lenin have entered into our political vocabulary.[1] Before he coins such a word, the speaker seems to go round and round as if searching for some central point. Then he finds it and as if placing a nail in position, glances round once more, lifts his hammer with great vigor and hits it on the head once, twice, three times, ten times, until the nail holds firmly, so firmly that it is hard to pull out even when no longer needed. When it is needed no longer, Lenin knocks it from the left, from the right, loosens it, draws it out, jokingly throws it on the pile of scrap-iron in the archives to the great regret of all those who have grown so much accustomed to it.

The speech is coming to an end. The balance sheet is drawn, the conclusions firmly grasped. The speaker looks like a workman who has sweated over his job but has finished it. From time to time he passes his hand over the bald head on which can be seen little beads of perspiration. The voice becomes muffled—like embers burning in a dying fire. This is the end. But one must not expect any brilliant crowning *finale* without which, one assumes, no speaker can leave the rostrum. Others cannot, but Lenin can. There is no rhetorical winding up; he finishes the sentence and—full stop. Sometimes his final sentence goes thus: "If we understand this, if we do that, then we are sure to vanquish"; or "That is what we should aim at, not in words but in deeds." Or, even more simply, "That is all I wanted to tell you." Such an ending, which accords well with the nature of Lenin's oratory and, generally, with his whole character, does not seem to dampen the enthusiasm of the audience. On the contrary. Precisely after an ending so gray and without effects, the crowd suddenly becomes aware

[1] *Translator's note:* Trotsky quotes here words like *khvostism*—"dragging after"; *peredyshka*—"breathing spell"; *smychka*—"a close alliance or harmonious union of workers and peasants"; *drachka*—"a squabble, a brawl"; *komchvanstvo*—"Communist boastfulness."

once again of all that Lenin gave it in his speech and bursts into stormy applause, grateful and enthusiastic.

But Lenin, already gathering his papers, hurriedly leaves the rostrum in order to escape the inevitable. His head withdrawn slightly into his shoulders, chin down, eyes hidden under the brows, his mustache bristling a little crossly on the upper lip pouting with annoyance. The roar of clapping grows, wave upon wave: "Long live . . . Lenin . . . leader . . . Ilyich . . ." Under the glow of electric lamps passes that unique head, surrounded on all sides by waves and waves of enthusiasm. And when it seems the storm has reached its zenith, breaking through the tumult and the clapping, a young voice, strained and happy, can be heard: *"Long live Lenin!"* Somewhere, from the inner depths of solidarity, of love, and enthusiasm, like a powerful hurricane there rises a tremendous cry, the call of the people shaking the vaults: "Long live Lenin!"

III. Essays, Articles, Speeches

1. Lenin's National Characteristics[1]

Lenin's internationalism need not be stressed. It found striking expression from the first days of the World War in his irreconcilable break with the counterfeit internationalism which dominated the Second International. The official leaders of "socialism" tried, from the height of the Parliamentary rostrum, to reconcile the interests of the fatherland with those of mankind, using abstract arguments in the style of old-time cosmopolitans. In practice this led to supporting the rapacious fatherland with the forces of the proletariat.

Lenin's internationalism is not a formula for harmonizing national and international interests with empty verbiage. It is a guide to revolutionary action embracing all nations. Our planet, inhabited by so-called civilized humanity, is considered as one single battlefield where various nations and social classes contend. The framework of one nation cannot contain in itself a single weighty problem; visible and invisible threads connect its very essence with dozens of events taking place in all corners of the world. In the evaluation of international phenomena and international forces, Lenin more than anybody else is free from the slightest national bias.

Marx maintained that the philosophers have sufficiently interpreted the world; now the real task was to change it. He,

[1] *Pravda,* April 23, 1920. On the occasion of Lenin's fiftieth anniversary.

the prophetic genius, did not live to see this fulfilled. The process of transformation of the old world is now in full swing, and Lenin is its first agent. His internationalism consisted in the practical appreciation of, and in the practical intervention in, historic events on a world scale and toward goals which embrace the whole world. Russia and her fate constitute only one element of a tremendous historical process, the outcome of which will decide the fate of humanity.

No, there is no need to authenticate Lenin's internationalism. And yet Lenin himself is a genuinely national type. He is deeply rooted in contemporary Russian history: He is the epitome of that history; he gives it its highest expression and precisely in this way he attains the pinnacle of international activity and of world influence.

To characterize Lenin's personality as "national" may, at first sight, seem unexpected; but on closer scrutiny it becomes self-evident. In order to be able to direct an upheaval on a scale unprecedented in the history of nations, the upheaval through which Russia has been passing, there needs to exist between the vital forces of the country and the leader some organic, indissoluble link deep down, at the roots of his being. Lenin embodies the Russian proletariat, politically a young social class which in age is scarcely older than Lenin himself. But that class is deeply national because all Russia's previous developments are bound up with it and on it depends the life and death of the Russian nation. Freedom from habit and custom, from hypocrisy and convention, boldness of thought, audacity in action—audacity which never becomes recklessness, are characteristic of the Russian proletariat—and of Lenin as well.

These qualities of the Russian proletariat, which actually make of it the most important force of international revolution, had arisen as a result of the whole course of Russian history, of the barbaric cruelty of autocracy, of the feebleness of the privileged classes, of the fitful development of capitalism in dependence on the world stock exchanges, of the hollowness of the Russian bourgeoisie with its decadent ideology and political mediocrity. Our "Third Estate" did not and could not go through its Reformation or its Great Revolution; so it became the destiny of the proletariat to confront all-embracing universal revolutionary tasks. Our history never produced a Luther, a Thomas Münzer, nor a Mirabeau, a Danton, or Robespierre. And this was precisely why the Russian proletariat had its Lenin. What was lacking in tradition was amply made up in the scale and sweep of the revolution.

Lenin reflects and represents the working class not only in its proletarian present-day character, but also in its recent peasant past. This indisputable leader of the proletariat has not only the outward look of a *muzhik,* but in his innermost being he was one. Outside the Smolny Institute a monument has been erected to another great figure of the world proletariat: Karl Marx stands there on a plinth of stone in a black frock coat. This is only a detail, of course, but even in one's imagination it is impossible to put Lenin into a black frock coat. On some portraits Marx is shown wearing some kind of white starched shirtfront on which dangles something like a monocle. That Marx was not inclined to foppishness is all too obvious to anybody who has the slightest idea of his work. But he was born and grew up in a different national-cultural background; he breathed a different air, as did other leading figures of the German working class, rooted not in peasant villages, but in guilds and corporations and in an elaborate urban culture following upon the Middle Ages.

The very style of Marx, rich and brilliant, combining vigor and flexibility, anger and irony, austerity and sophistication, is marked by all the literary and aesthetic heritage of German political and social writings which go back to the Reformation and beyond. Lenin's literary and oratorical style is extremely simple, utilitarian, spare, as is his whole nature. But in this powerful asceticism there is not a trace of moralizing. This is not a matter of principle, nor a preconceived and worked out system, nor is it, of course, posturing. It is simply the outward expression of an inner concentration of forces, a concentration for action. It is the practical husbandry of a *muzhik* —only on an immense scale.

The whole of Marx can be found in *The Communist Manifesto,* in the preface to his *Critique,* and in *Das Kapital.* Even if he were not the founder of the First International, he would forever remain what he had been till now. Not so Lenin, whose whole personality is centered in revolutionary action. His scientific works were only the preliminaries to action. If he had never published a single book, he would forever have entered history just as he did: as a leader of the proletarian revolution, a founder of the Third International.

A clear and scientific system, dialectical materialism, was indispensable for the historical sweep of his action; it was indispensable, but it was not sufficient. What was also needed was that deep creative force which we call intuition: the ability to judge events rapidly, at a glance, to distinguish the essential from the trivial, to fill up imaginatively the missing parts of the picture, to think out other people's thoughts to the end, and in the first instance the enemy's thoughts; to combine all these disparate elements into one totality and to strike a blow straightway while the very "idea" of the blow was still shaping itself in one's mind. This is the intuition of action. This is what we call in Russian true sagacity.

When Lenin, screwing up his left eye, listens over the radio to a Parliamentary speech by one of the imperialist politicians, or to a text of a diplomatic note of immediate interest, a note in which bloody perfidy vies with the most affable hypocrisy, he looks like a shrewd *muzhik* not to be taken in by smooth words and fooled by polite phrases. Such is the sagacity of the peasant, but in this case heightened to a supreme degree, reaching the peak of greatness and armed with all the latest achievements of scientific thought.

The young Russian proletariat could accomplish its tremendous deed only by dragging along with it the peasantry, that heavy lump of rural Russia's sodden earth, stuck fast to its roots. Our national past was leading up to this. But just because history pushed the proletariat to power, our revolution could, in one movement and so radically, overcome the limitations and backward provincialism of our national past. Soviet Russia has become not only the refuge of the Communist International; she is the living expression of its program and its method.

By the unknown ways in which human personality is shaped, ways as yet unrevealed by science, Lenin absorbed from the national environment all that he needed to perform the greatest revolutionary act in history. Precisely because in Lenin the socialist revolution, for long elaborated theoretically on an international scale, found for the first time its national realization, he became, in the most direct and most immediate sense, the leader of the international world proletariat.

Such is Lenin today, the day of his fiftieth birthday.

2. *The Philistine and the Revolutionary*

In one of the many anthologies on Lenin I found an essay by the English writer H. G. Wells under the title "The Dreamer in the Kremlin." [1] The editors of the volume remark in the preface that "even such progressive people as Wells had not understood the meaning of the proletarian revolution which occurred in Russia."

This, it would seem, was not a sufficient reason for includ-

[1] *Translator's note:* See *The Sunday Express*, November 28, 1920.

ing Wells' essay in a volume devoted to the leader of that revolution. But I do not want to be quarrelsome; in any case I
personally have read not without interest Wells' few pages.
This, however, as will be seen later, has not been due to the
author.

I vividly remember Wells' visit in Moscow. This was during
the cold and hungry winter of 1920–21. There was in the air
an anxious presentiment of the difficulties which awaited us in
the spring. Starving Moscow lay buried in thick snow. The
economic policy was on the eve of a sharp change. I remember very well the impression which the talk with Wells made
on Lenin: "What a *petit bourgeois!* What a Philistine!" he
kept repeating, raising both his arms, laughing and sighing in
a way characteristic of him when he felt ashamed for another
man. "Oh, what a Philistine!" he repeated, recalling the conversation.

We were both waiting for the opening of a session of the
Politbureau, and in fact Lenin said nothing more about Wells,
except what I have just quoted. But this was quite enough. I
admit I have read little of Wells, and I have never met him.
But I could well imagine the personality of this English draw-
ing-room socialist, one of the Fabians, a novelist, and the
author of fantastic and utopian stories, who had journeyed to
Moscow to take a look at the Communist experiment. Lenin's
exclamations, and quite especially their tone, completed and
enlivened the picture.

Now, Wells' essay, which providence in its mysterious ways
introduced into a Lenin anthology, not only evoked in my
memory Lenin's exclamation, but filled it with living content.
Although there is hardly a trace of Lenin in Wells' essay about
him, there is in it the whole of Wells himself seen as clearly
as the back of one's hand.

Let us start from the beginning, from the first complaint
made by Wells: poor man, do you know it took him quite
some time and some effort to get an appointment with Lenin

and this was "tedious and irritating" to him. Why should it have been? Had Lenin invited Wells there? Did he promise to see him? Perhaps Lenin had too much time on his hands? On the contrary, during these difficult days every minute of Lenin's time was taken up; it was not easy for him to carve out one hour in which to receive Wells. This should have been plain even to a foreigner. The trouble was that Wells, as an illustrious foreigner, and, for all his "socialism" a rather conservative Englishman of imperialist habits, was absolutely convinced that in fact he was by his visit conferring a great honor on this barbarian country and its leader. His whole article, from first to last, oozes this quite groundless conviction.

The characterization of Lenin begins, as one might have expected, from a great discovery. You see, Lenin "is not a writer." Who, in fact, should know this better than Wells, a professional man of letters? "The shrill little pamphlets and papers issued from Moscow in his name, full of misconceptions of the labor psychology of the West . . . hardly display anything of the real Lenin's mentality. . . ." The honorable gentleman does not know, of course, that Lenin is the author of a whole series of fundamental works on the agrarian question, on economic theory, on sociology and philosophy. Wells knew only the "shrill little pamphlets"; he also remarked that they were issued "in his name," hinting perhaps that they were written by other people. The real "Lenin mentality" reveals itself not in the dozens of volumes which he had written, but in the hour-long conversation into which the eminent visitor from Great Britain so generously deigned to enter.

One would have expected Wells to give at least an interesting description of Lenin's physiognomy. For a single well-observed, well-rendered feature we would have been ready to forgive him all his Fabian trivialities. But there is nothing of the kind in the essay.

"Lenin has a pleasant, quick-changing brownish [!] face with a lively smile." . . . Lenin "is not very like the photographs you see of him . . . he gesticulated a little with his hands during our conversation . . ." Wells did not go beyond the banalities of a commonplace reporter, who has to fill a column of his capitalist paper. In addition Wells discovered that Lenin's head resembled the "domed and slightly one-sided cranium" of Arthur Balfour, and that, generally speaking, Lenin is a "little man: his feet scarcely touch the ground as he sits on the edge of his chair." As far as Arthur Balfour's skull is concerned, we can say nothing about this worthy object, and we are ready to believe that it is domed. But all the rest! What indecent trash! Lenin had a reddish-blond complexion and one could not by any means describe him as "brownish." He was of medium height, or a little below that; but that he looked a "little man," whose feet hardly reached the floor, might have been only the impression of a Wells who arrived feeling like a civilized Gulliver on a journey to the land of northern Communist Lilliputians. Wells also noticed that Lenin, whenever there was a pause in the conversation, was "screwing up one eye"; this habit, explains the shrewd writer, "is due perhaps to some defect in focussing." We know this gesture of Lenin's well. It was always there when Lenin had before him a stranger with whom he had nothing in common. Covering his eyes, he used to throw a rapid glance through his fingers and the "defect in focussing" consisted in no more than that he saw through his interlocutor, saw his self-satisfied vanity, his narrow-mindedness, his "civilized" conceit, and his "civilized" ignorance. Long afterward, remembering the occasion, Lenin would shake his head: "What a Philistine! What an awful *petit bourgeois!*"

Comrade Rothstein was present during the talk, and Wells *en passant* made the discovery that this fact was "characteristic for the present condition of Russian affairs." Rothstein, you see, controls Lenin on behalf of the Commissariat of Foreign Affairs in view of Lenin's extreme frankness and his "dreamer's imprudence." What can one say about such a priceless observation? Wells went to the Kremlin, his mind stuffed with all the rubbishy information purveyed by the international bourgeoisie and with his penetrating eye—without any "defect of focussing"—found in Lenin's office the confirmation of what he had earlier fished out of the pages of *The Times* or from some other source of respectable and genteel gossip.

But what then was the conversation about?

Here Wells conveys to us some hopeless platitudes which only show what a pitiful and hollow echo Lenin's thought evokes in some other heads whose one-sidedness incidentally we have no reason to question.

Wells turned up "expecting to struggle with a doctrinaire Marxist," but in fact he "found nothing of the sort." This should not surprise us. We have already learned that "the real Lenin mentality" has been revealed not during the more than thirty years of his political and literary activity, but in his conversation with the citizen from England. "I had been told that Lenin lectured people; he certainly did not do so on this occasion." How, indeed, to lecture a "gentleman" [2] so full of self-importance? That Lenin liked to lecture people or to teach them was quite untrue. It was true that one could learn a good deal from a conversation with him. But this happened only when Lenin was of the opinion that his interlocutor was able to learn something. In such cases Lenin spared neither time nor effort. After two or three minutes in the company of the wonderful Gulliver who by a lucky chance found himself in the office of the "little man," Lenin must have become firmly convinced that the inscription at the entry to Dante's hell "Abandon all hope!" was quite appropriate in this situation.

The conversation touched upon the problem of big cities. Precisely in Russia, as Wells himself said, a remarkable idea occurred to him, namely, that the outlook of a city is determined by the trade in the shops and in the marketplaces. He shared this revelation with Lenin. Lenin "admitted" that under

[2] *Translator's note:* The English word is used in the text.

Communism cities might become much smaller. Wells "pointed out" to Lenin that the renovation of cities and towns would constitute a gigantic task and that quite a few of the enormous buildings of Petersburg would retain their significance only as historical monuments. Lenin agreed with this original platitude. "I think it warmed his heart," added Wells, "to find someone who understood a necessary consequence of collectivism that even many of his own people fail to grasp."

Well, this gives you the measure of Wells' level of thinking. He treats as proof of his extraordinary perspicacity the discovery that under a Communist regime the existing huge urban concentrations will disappear and that our present monsters of capitalist architecture will preserve their significance as historic monuments only (unless they will be granted the honor of being demolished). Of course, how would poor Communists ("the tiresome class-war fanatics") arrive at such discoveries, which, by the way, have a long time ago been described in a popular addendum to the old program of the German Social Democratic Party. We shall not mention that all this was quite familiar to the classical utopians of socialism.

Now you will understand, I hope, why Wells did not at all notice Lenin's famous laughter about which he had been told so much. Lenin was in no mood to laugh. I even fear that he might have been a victim of quite the opposite temptation. But his versatile and clever hand, as usual, rendered him a service by concealing just in time an unkind yawn from a visitor preoccupied with his own person.

As you have learned, Lenin did not lecture Wells—for reasons which seem to us quite obvious. In return, however, Wells persisted in giving Lenin advice. He kept on impressing upon Lenin the completely new idea that for the success of socialism it is necessary to change not only the material side of life but also "the mentality of a whole people." He drew Lenin's attention to the fact that "The Russians are by habit and tradition traders and individualists"; he also explained to him that Communism "was pressing too hard and too fast, and destroying before it was ready to rebuild," and so on, and so forth, all in the same spirit. "And that," relates Wells, "brought us to our essential difference—the difference of the Collectivist and the Marxist." By "evolutionary collectivism" one should recognize a brew of the Fabians which consists of liberalism, philanthropy, a stingy social legislation together with Sunday meditations about a brighter future. Wells himself thus formulates the essence of "evolutionary collectivism": "I believe that through a vast sustained educational campaign the existing capitalist system could be civilized into a Collectivist world system." Wells does not make it clear, however, who is going to introduce this "vast sustained educational campaign" and who will be subjected to it: Are we to suppose that English "milords" with "domed" heads will exercise it over the English proletariat, or, on the contrary, that the English proletariat will subject "milords' " heads to this education? Oh, no, anything but the latter. For what purpose do we have in this world the educated Fabians, the intellectuals, with their altruistic imagination, the gentlemen and the ladies, the Messrs. Wells and the Mesdames Snowdens, if not that they should, by a planned and prolonged process of sharing what they themselves carry concealed in their own heads, civilize capitalist society and transform it into a collectivist one, with such a sensible and happy gradualness that even the British monarchy will not notice this transformation?

All this Wells went on expounding to Lenin, and Lenin sat listening. "For me," graciously remarked Wells, "it was very refreshing" to talk to "this amazing little man." And for Lenin? —oh, long-suffering Ilyich! He certainly had quite a few expressive and racy Russian words on his tongue. He did not utter them aloud nor did he translate them into English, not only because his English vocabulary would not stretch that far, but also because he was much too polite. But he could not limit himself to a polite silence alone.

"He [Lenin] had to argue . . ." relates Wells, "that modern capitalism is incurably predatory, wasteful and unteachable." Lenin quoted facts and figures published, *inter alia,* in the new book of Chiozza Money, and showed how capitalism destroyed the English shipyards, how it prevented a sensible exploitation of coal resources, and so on. Lenin knew the language of facts and figures. "I had, I will confess," unexpectedly concluded Mr. Wells, "a very uphill argument." What did this mean? Wasn't this the beginning of a capitulation of the evolutionary collectivism before the logic of Marxism? No, no. "Abandon all hope."

This admission, which on first sight seems unexpected, is not at all fortuitous, but forms an integral part of the typically Fabian evolutionary and didactic system. It was, in fact, addressed to the English capitalists, bankers, peers, and their ministers. Wells was telling them: You see, you behave so stupidly, so greedily, so selfishly, that you make it extremely difficult for me to defend the principles of my evolutionary collectivism in the discussions with the dreamer in the Kremlin. Listen to reason, take part in the Fabians' Sunday ritual ablutions, civilize yourself, march onto the road of progress.

Wells' melancholy admission was not the beginning of a critical revision of his views, but a continuation of that educative work of the same capitalist society, which after the imperialist war and the Versailles Treaty, has so much improved, so much moralized and fabianized itself.

Not without condescending sympathy, Wells remarks that Lenin "has an unlimited confidence in his work." With this statement we shall not quarrel. Indeed, Lenin had faith enough in the justice of his cause. What is true is true. This faith was also, incidentally, the source of the patience with which Lenin entered into conversations, during these harsh months of the blockade, with any foreigner who could serve as a contact, albeit indirectly, between Russia and the West. So Lenin met Wells. He talked a quite different language with

English workers who used to visit him. With them he entered into a lively exchange; he taught them and he learned from them. With Wells the intercourse could not have anything but a strained, diplomatic character. "Our . . . argumentation ended indecisively," sums up the author. In other words, the match between evolutionary collectivism and Marxism this time ended in a draw. Wells returned to Great Britain, Lenin remained in the Kremlin. Wells wrote up his pompous "correspondence" for his bourgeois public, and Lenin, shaking his head, kept on repeating: "What a *petit bourgeois!* Aye, aye, what a Philistine!"

One may ask why and for what purpose I have given so much attention to an insignificant article by H. G. Wells, four years after its publication. The fact that the article was included in one of the anthologies brought out in connection with Lenin's death is not a valid reason. Nor is it a sufficient justification to say that I wrote these lines in Sukhum, where I was undergoing medical treatment. I had more serious considerations.

Just now in England, Wells' party is in power. At the head of the party we see the enlightened representatives of evolutionary collectivism. It seemed to me—perhaps not quite unreasonably—that Wells' words devoted to Lenin may perhaps better than anything else reveal to us the spirit of the leaders of the English Labour Party. After all, Wells was by no means the worst of them.

How terribly these people lag behind, pressed down by the leaden weight of their bourgeois prejudices. Their pride, which is nothing else but a time-worn reflex of their historical role in the past, prevents them from penetrating, as they should, the minds of other nations, from examining new ideological phenomena, new historical processes which all pass them by. Routine-ridden, narrow-minded empiricists, with blinkers of their bourgeois public opinion over their eyes, these gentlemen carry with them all over the world their own prejudices; they have a peculiar talent for noticing nothing around them except themselves. Lenin had lived in various countries of Europe, had learned foreign languages, read, studied, listened, pondered matters deeply, compared, generalized. At the head of a great revolutionary country, he never missed an opportunity to inform himself, attentively and conscientiously, to inquire, to learn. He never ceased to follow the events of the entire world. He read and spoke German, French, and English fluently, and he could read Italian too. In the last years of his life, overloaded with work, stealthily, during the Politbureau's meetings, he studied a Czechoslovak grammar in order to have a more direct contact with the working movement of that country. Sometimes we used to "catch him out," and, embarrassed, he would laugh and try to excuse himself. Beside him Wells was the embodiment of those pseudo-educated, narrow-minded bourgeois who look without seeing, who do not want to learn anything because they feel so comfortable behind their barrier of inherited prejudices. Then you have Mr. MacDonald, a more solid and gloomy variety of the same type, reassuring public opinion in England: We have fought against Moscow and we have won.

Have *they* won? They are indeed poor "little men" even if they have grown tall in size. Even now, after all that has happened, they still have no inkling of what the future has in store for them. Liberal and conservative businessmen easily manipulate these pedantic "evolutionary" socialists now in power, deliberately preparing not only the downfall of their government but their political debacle as well. At the same time, however, unknowingly, they prepare the path to power for English Marxists. Yes, precisely for the Marxists, for those "tiresome class war fanatics." The English social revolution too will proceed according to the laws defined by Marx.

Wells, with his peculiar humor so much like a stodgy English pudding, once threatened to cut off Marx's "doctrinaire" head of hair and his beard, to anglicize him, to make him more respectable and to "fabianize" him. But nothing came of this project, and nothing will ever come of it. Marx will remain Marx, just as Lenin will remain Lenin, even after subjection to Wells' blunt razor blade for more than a full tiresome hour. We dare to venture a forecast that in the not too distant future in London, perhaps in Trafalgar Square, there will appear, next to each other, two monuments in bronze: one of Karl Marx and the other of Vladimir Lenin. And English workers will say to their children: "What a good thing it was, that the little men of the Labour Party did not manage either to cut the hair or to shave the beards of these two giants."

Awaiting this day, which I hope to be alive to see, I shut my eyes for a second and I see clearly Lenin's figure in the same chair in which Wells saw him, and I hear—after Wells' visit or perhaps a day later—the slightly mournful yet good-natured voice: "What a *petit bourgeois!* What a Philistine!"

April 6, 1924

3. The True and the False[1]

(On Lenin's portrait by Gorky)

"It is difficult to draw his portrait," says Gorky of Lenin. This is correct. Gorky's writings about Lenin are very poor. The fabric of his description seems to be woven of various kinds of yarn. Now and again there passes a thin thread more brilliant than the others and one feels the artistic sensitivity

[1] *Translator's note:* This essay is from *Pravda* of October 7, 1924, where it was first published; it is not included in the first Russian edition of Trotsky's book.

behind it. But there are many more threads of banal psychological analysis, and one notices all too frequently the very *petit bourgeois* moralist. As a whole, the tissue is not too beautiful. But as Gorky was the weaver, his *oeuvre* will be examined for a long time to come. This is why it should be discussed. Perhaps we shall find an opportunity to better understand, or to better notice, certain characteristics, large or small, of Lenin's personality.

Gorky is right when he says that Lenin is the extraordinary and perfect embodiment of a tense will striving toward the goal. This *tension toward the goal* is Lenin's essential characteristic. I have said this before and shall come back to it again. But when, a little further, Gorky treats Lenin as "one of the righteous," this sounds false and is in bad taste. The expression "the righteous," borrowed from the Church, from the language of religious sects with the odor of Lent and the oil of holy icons, does not accord with Lenin at all. He was a great man, a magnificent giant, and nothing human was alien to him. During one Congress of the Soviets there came to the rostrum a fairly well-known representative of a religious sect, a Communist Christian (or something of the kind), very clever and cunning. He straightway intoned a psalm praising Lenin as the Father, the giver of all good things. I remember that Vladimir Ilyich, sitting at the table with other members of the Presidium, lifted his head, as if a little frightened, then turned slightly toward us and whispered, very angrily, to those nearest to him: "What are all these obscenities?"

The word "obscenity" escaped him quite unexpectedly, as if unwittingly, and yet it was the right word. I was controlling my laughter; I was savoring Lenin's incomparable and spontaneous description of the praises sung by the very Christian speaker. Well, Gorky's expression "the righteous" has something in common with the "Father-the-giver-of-all-good-things" of the pious man. It is, if you allow me to say so, an "obscenity" on a small scale.

What came later was even worse:

"For me Lenin is a legendary hero, a man who tore from his breast a flaming heart to lift it like a torch and to light men's way . . ."

Brrrr. How horrid. It reminds one of the old Izerghill (I think this was the name of the old witch so popular in the days of our youth) and the story of her relations with the gypsy Danko. In that story, if I am not mistaken, there is also a heart which changes into a torch. Or is it in some opera . . . ? Yes, I mean an *opera*: with decor imitating a southern landscape, with the lighting of fireworks and a gypsy band. Yet in Lenin's personality there is nothing which could possibly suggest an opera and even less of anything that can bring to mind the romanticism of itinerant gypsies. Lenin is a man from Simbirsk, from "Piter," [2] of Moscow, of the world—a hard realist, a professional revolutionary. There could be nothing in common between Danko, the hero of the fable, and Lenin who disparaged romanticism, theatrical pretense, and bohemian revolutionism. Those who are in need of revolutionary models borrowed from gypsy tales should rather look for them in the history of Social Revolutionaries.

Then, three lines down, Gorky adds:

"Lenin was as simple and as straightforward as all that he was saying."

If it were so, then why should we imagine him tearing out a flaming heart from his breast? In such a gesture there would be no simplicity, no sincerity . . . But these two words "simple" and "straightforward" are not chosen with great felicity; they are much too commonplace and plain. One uses these terms to describe an honest young lad, a brave soldier, who babbles "plain truth" whatever it might be. These terms do not fit Lenin at all, no matter how we understand them.

Certainly, he had the simplicity of a genius in the way he took decisions, in the conclusions he reached, in his methods,

---

[2] *Translator's note:* Abbreviation of Petersburg.

in his activity: He knew how to reject, to push aside, to disregard all that had no real importance, all that was only incidental or superficial; he knew how to reach the heart of the matter, how to reduce a problem to its essentials.

But all this does not mean that he was just "simple" and "straightforward." Even less does it mean that his thought followed a "straight line," as Gorky maintains somewhere else —a most regrettable expression, worthy indeed of a *petit bourgeois* and a Menshevik.

In connection with this I suddenly remembered a definition given by the writer Bebel who spoke about "the complex curve of Lenin's straight line." Contrary to the first impression these words make, and in spite of the antinomy and the overelaborate subtlety of the juxtaposition, the definition is nevertheless correct. In any case, it is immeasurably better than the "straightforwardness" used by Gorky. A man who is just "simple" and "straightforward" marches straight toward his goal. Lenin marched and led toward one and the same goal by indirect and often very roundabout ways. Last but not least, the two adjectives put together—"simple and straightforward"—give not the slightest idea of Lenin's inimitable slyness, his quick and brilliant ingenuity, the passion of a virtuoso with which he delighted in tripping his adversary and seeing him fall, or in enmeshing him into a trap.

We have already mentioned Lenin's singleness of purpose, his tense striving toward the goal. On this characteristic we should dwell a little longer. One critic, believing he had discovered a deep truth, started explaining to me that Lenin distinguished himself not only by this tenseness of will with which he pursued his goal, but also by his dexterity as a tactician. The same critic reproached me that in the portrait I had given of Lenin, stressing the rocklike hardness of the great man, I had failed to emphasize his suppleness.

The critic who had thus taken me to task, though he differed from Gorky, did not understand the relative weight and meaning of words either. Indeed, it is extremely difficult to make people aware that "the tenseness in striving toward the goal" does not necessarily imply marching "in a straight line." And what would Lenin's suppleness be worth without this tenseness which did not flag even for a moment?

In this world one finds as much political suppleness as one wants: Bourgeois Parliamentarism is an excellent school in which politicians are constantly trained in flexibility, where they constantly learn how to bend the backbone. If Lenin had very often mocked "the straight line of the doctrinaires," he had just as often showed contempt for those who are too supple, too flexible, those who bow down not necessarily, and not always, before their bourgeois masters, not indeed in order to derive some advantage—but, say, before the pressure of public opinion, or in the face of a difficult situation—just taking the line of least resistance.

The very essence of Lenin, all his most inward worth, consists precisely in this: that always and everywhere he was pursuing his unique goal, the importance of which he felt so deeply that it became as if organically his, it became part of himself—he was at one with the aim he was pursuing, and there was no means of drawing a line between his person and his purpose. He could not view people, books, events, otherwise than through the prism of this unique purpose of his existence.

It is impossible to sum up a man in one word. To say that he was "great" or that he was a "genius" really means nothing. But if I were to attempt briefly to define what sort of man Lenin was, I would stress that his whole being was geared to one great purpose. He possessed *the tenseness of striving toward* his goal.

Gorky remarks on Lenin's captivating laughter. "The laughter of a man who, perceiving so clearly the whole weight of human stupidity and the acrobatic tricks of reason, was able to delight in the childlike artlessness of those of simple hearts."

Expressed somewhat laboriously, this is substantially correct. Lenin laughed at stupid and malicious people who tried to be clever; and he laughed with the tolerance justified by his enormous superiority. Some of those nearest to Lenin laughed with him though not always for the same reasons . . . But the laughter of the masses always accorded well with his. He liked those of "simple hearts" (to use the evangelical expression). Gorky describes how, in Capri, Lenin learned the art of fishing from Italian fishermen. These good people explained to him: tug fast when the rod makes "drin, drin." As soon as Lenin, feeling the pull of the hook, caught his first fish, he exclaimed with *childish joy,* with the *enthusiasm of a real beginner:* "Oho, drin, drin!"

This is excellent. Here is a truly living bit of Lenin. This passion, this rapture, this tense will to achieve his aim, to "tug fast" and get his prey—"Oho, drin, drin! That's it! There it is!"

How far all this is from the Righteous, Lent, the Giver-of-all-good-things which we have quoted. This is the true Lenin, a living part of him. When Lenin, catching a fish, shouts his enthusiasm, we guess his lively delight in nature, in everything that is near nature, in children, in animals, in music. His powerful thinking mechanism was not far removed from what is *outside* thought, outside conscious brain work—it was not far removed from the primitive and the unspoken. Precisely what cannot be put into words is expressed by "drin, drin." For giving us this memorable detail, we should be prepared to forgive Gorky a quarter of all the banalities spread over his whole essay. It will be seen later on that we cannot, however, forgive him more than a quarter . . .

"He caressed children with great tenderness," Gorky tells us, "stroking them lightly with extreme delicacy." This is also well said; it shows us the man's affection which goes together with the respect, physical and moral, for the child's personality. One would notice the same in Lenin's handshake—vigorous and yet gentle.

Lenin's attitude to animals I remember best from the following episode:

We were holding a meeting in the mountain village of Zimmerwald, and our commission was charged with preparing a manifesto. We were sitting at a round table in the open air. Not far away under the tap stood a large vat full of water. Just before our meeting (which was arranged rather early in the morning) a few delegates washed themselves under that tap. I saw Fritz Platten plunging head first and up to his waist into the water as if he were out to drown himself, to the great consternation of the other participants in the conference.

The work of the commission took a distressing turn. There were disagreements on various points, but mainly between Lenin and the majority. At that moment two splendid dogs came into the garden. I do not know what kind of dogs they were—at that time I knew nothing of the breeding of dogs. They must have belonged to the owner of the place, because they started playing peacefully on the sand in the morning sunshine. Vladimir Ilyich suddenly got up and left the table. Half-kneeling, he started laughing and tickling, first one dog then the other, under their ears, along their bellies, lightly, delicately (to use Gorky's expression). There was spontaneity in Lenin's gesture. One is tempted to say that he behaved like a little urchin, so carefree, so boyish was his laughter. He glanced at our commission as if he wanted to invite the comrades to take part in this lovely diversion. It seemed to me that people looked with some astonishment: Everybody was still preoccupied by the serious debate. Lenin went on stroking the animals, but in a less ebullient manner. He then returned to the table and refused to sign the proposed text of the manifesto. The discussion began anew with fresh violence. It occurs to me now that it was quite possible that Lenin was in need of "diversion" in order to weigh in his mind the arguments for and against the decision to sign. But he did not act with any premeditation; his subconscious and his conscious thought worked in complete harmony.

Gorky admired in Lenin "this youthful ardor which went into all he did." This ardor was disciplined and dominated by an iron will, just as a mountain stream is kept in check by its granite banks. Gorky did not seem to notice this, but his remark is nevertheless true. There was in Lenin this "youthful ardor" and also "the unique spiritual courage of those who are profoundly, unshakably sure of their purpose." This, again, is well said and shrewdly observed. But, in other instances, the fusty and flabby language, the odor of sanctity or the "asceticism" (!) or "monkish heroism" (!!) do not at all accord with the youthful ardor—they just mix like fire and water. "Sanctity" and "asceticism" are characteristic of a man who devotes himself to the service of a "superior" spiritual principle, of a man who goes against his leanings and has to tame his personal passions. His asceticism is calculated because he expects to be rewarded for it. Lenin in his historical task was fulfilling himself completely and absolutely.

"The omniscient eyes of a great sly fox"—this is not bad, though formulated somewhat coarsely. But how can one have such eyes and at the same time be "simple," "straightforward," and, above all, have that aura of "sanctity"?

"He was fun-loving," Gorky tells us further, "and he laughed with all his body, truly overwhelmed with gaiety, he sometimes laughed literally to tears." This was true and was known by all that came into contact with him. At some gatherings at which there were not many people, Lenin would sometimes have a fit of laughter, and that happened not only when things went well, but even during hard and difficult moments. He tried to control himself as long as he could, but finally he would burst out with a peal of laughter which infected all the others. He forced himself to be quiet, to conceal his merriment, sometimes even bending down under the table, anxious not to disorganize the meeting. Such hilarity used to take hold of him especially when he was tired. I remember the familiar gesture. Moving his arm up and down, he was as if driving away the temptation. All in vain. He devised only one method of controlling himself: He would fix his gaze on his watch with the greatest concentration, carefully avoiding other people's eyes, and he would put on an extremely severe expression—in this way, with an affected stiffness, he would maintain the calmness befitting a chairman. In such cases it was the comrades' point of honor to "catch the eye of the speaker" and to provoke, by some jest, a relapse into hilarity. If they succeeded, the chairman was furious both with the culprit and with himself.

Of course, such diversions did not occur very often; when they did, it was usually toward the end of the session, after four or five hours of intense work, when everybody was exhausted. Normally, Ilyich used to conduct debates with the utmost strictness, and it was due to this method that we were able to dispose of innumerable problems during a single session.

"He had this particular expressive way of murmuring 'hm, hm,' " continues Gorky, "and he could invest this 'hm, hm' with an infinite gamut of meaning from biting irony to doubt and circumspection; and often this 'hm, hm' expressed a sharp sense of humor, noticed and understood only by the discerning and wise, who knew the devilish absurdities of existence." This is true and very correct. The "hm, hm" played indeed an important role in Lenin's conversations with those who were closest to him, and also in his controversies. He pronounced his "hm, hm" very clearly, each sound separately—"H-m, h-m"—and, as Gorky rightly says, with an infinite variety of nuances. It constituted a kind of signaling code which he used to express a great wealth of different feelings and moods. On paper "hm, hm" means nothing; in a personal talk it is endowed with a multitude of shades and acquires value by the tone of voice, by the movement of the head, by the flicker of the eyebrows, and by the eloquent gesture of the hands.

Gorky describes also Lenin's favorite posture:

"He would throw his head backwards, then to the side over the shoulder, would stick his thumbs into the armholes of his waistcoat under the armpits. There was in this posture something astonishingly funny and charming, one would say a victorious cock—and at such moments he was radiant."

All this is quite well said, except for that "victorious cock" which in no way fits Lenin's image. But the posture is excellently depicted. Alas! Let us read further:

"The great child of this sinful world, the wonderful man who felt the need to sacrifice himself, to offer himself as the victim of hostility and hatred in order to bring about the labor of love and beauty . . ." Please, Alexei Maximovich, have pity. . . . ". . . Child of this sinful world . . ." Oh! the pharisaic odor of this sentence! Often Lenin's manner was strikingly engaging, sometimes malicious, but there was nothing hypocritical about him. ". . . To offer himself as victim . . ." No, this is false, untrue, unbearably false! It jars on one's ears like a screw scraping on glass.

Lenin did not sacrifice himself. On the contrary, he lived a full life, a wonderfully abundant life, developing, expanding his whole personality, serving a cause which he himself freely chose. And his labor was not that of "love and beauty"—such high-flown and well-worn words mean nothing. Only capital letters are missing here: Love and Beauty. No, Lenin's task, which he took upon himself, was that of awakening and uniting the oppressed, so that they could free themselves from oppression—and this was the cause of ninety-nine percent of humanity.

Gorky tells us about Lenin's attentiveness toward his comrades, about his solicitude for their health, and so on. And adds: "In this watchfulness I never detected the kind of selfish preoccupation which an intelligent boss shows toward his honest and efficient workers."

Well, here Gorky was completely wrong, because he completely missed one of Lenin's main characteristics. The personal attentiveness which Lenin showed his comrades was never devoid of the solicitude of a good boss who always bears in mind the work to be done. Of course, one cannot speak about "selfishness," because there was nothing selfish in his preoccupation. Lenin's personal attentiveness toward his comrades was dictated by his devotion to the cause—precisely to the same cause for which the comrades themselves gathered around him; about this there can be no doubt. This attention which Lenin gave to them both as his co-workers and as individuals, in no way detracts from his humanity. It only testifies once again to his singleness of purpose, to the tenseness with which his whole personality was geared to the achievement of his aim.

Gorky, who did not notice this, was certainly unable to understand why Lenin reacted as he did to Gorky's innumerable intercessions in favor of people who had "suffered" in the revolution. As we all know, there were many victims of the revolution; there were also very many appeals in their favor which Gorky addressed directly to Lenin. Some of these were indeed ridiculous. It is enough to recall his fantastically insistent intervention in defense of the Social Revolutionaries during the famous trial in Moscow. Gorky relates: "I do not remember a single case in which Lenin had refused my request. If it happened that Lenin's directives were not followed, this was no doubt not his fault, but the result of those accursed 'technical defects' which were always so numerous in our governmental machinery. There was also plain ill-will on the part of some people who simply did not want to help, and did not care to save lives. . . ."

We must admit that this statement by Gorky shocked us more than anything else. What does all this suggest? Does it mean that Lenin, as the leader of the party and the head of the state, persecuted mercilessly all the enemies of the revolution, but that Gorky's intervention was a sufficient reason for him to relent? That there was "not a single case" in which Lenin refused the writer's request? That the fate of men was settled by a friendly chat with Lenin? This assertion would have been quite incomprehensible, if it were not for Gorky's remark that his intercessions were not always effective. For this he blames the "technical defects" of the governmental machinery. Was this really so? Was Lenin really so helpless as to be unable to overcome these "defects" in a simple matter of releasing a prisoner, or sparing somebody punishment? This is extremely dubious. Would it not be more logical to assume that Lenin, having glanced at the petition and at the petitioner with his "omniscient eyes of a great sly fox," just avoided entering into a discussion with Gorky, entrusting to the Soviet machinery, with all its defects real and imaginary, the question of acting in the best interests of the revolution? Indeed, Lenin was not all that "simple" and all that "straightforward" when he had to defend himself against the *petit bourgeois* sentimentality. True, Lenin's respect for human personality was enormous, but it was also subordinated to his respect and solicitude for mankind as a whole, which in our epoch means in the first instance the world proletariat. If Vladimir Ilyich had been unable to subordinate the particular to the general, he might have indeed been one of the Righteous who offered himself as a martyr in the cause of Love and Beauty, but he would not by any means have been Lenin the leader of the Bolshevik Party and of the October Revolution.

It is in the light of what I have just said that one should understand the "extraordinary stubbornness" with which, according to Gorky, Lenin for over a year insisted that Gorky should go abroad for medical treatment. "In Europe, in a good sanatorium you will undergo a cure and you will be able to do three times as much work as here. Aye, aye! Go abroad, take care of your health, please, go. Don't be obstinate."

The warm sympathy which Lenin had for Gorky, for the man as well as for the writer, was unmistakable and widely known. No doubt, Gorky's poor health worried Vladimir Ilyich. Nonetheless, in his stubborn insistence that Gorky should go abroad there was also a political motive. In Russia, during these difficult years, Gorky was getting hopelessly confused and might have gone tragically astray; abroad, looking at capitalism and its civilization, he was more likely to find his bearings, to recover the mood which once in the past had made him "spit in the face" of bourgeois France. Incidentally, it would have been unnecessary for him to repeat this quite meaningless "demonstration." But the feeling behind this instinctive gesture was much more productive than the soul-saving intercessions on behalf of those workers in the field of "culture" whose sufferings were due only to the fact that they, poor people, did not manage to tighten the hangman's noose around the neck of the proletarian revolution in time.

Of course, Lenin took great care of Gorky. Of course, he sincerely desired that Gorky should recover his health, that he should live and work. But he needed a "straightened out" Gorky. That was why he stubbornly insisted on sending him abroad to get again a whiff of capitalist culture. Even if one knew nothing about the background to this relationship, one could easily have inferred Lenin's motives from Gorky himself. Lenin acted indeed like an "intelligent boss" who never and in no circumstances loses sight of the good of the cause entrusted to him by history.

It was not as a revolutionary writer but as a *petit bourgeois* moralizer that Gorky sketched the portrait of Lenin. As a result the figure of Vladimir Ilyich, so exceptional in its unity, breaks up on Gorky's canvas.

But things look even worse when the writer discusses poli-

tics in the proper sense of the word. Here in every sentence
there is either misunderstanding or plain falsehood. "A man
of extraordinary willpower, he was in all other respects a typical Russian intellectual."

Lenin—a "typical Russian intellectual"? Isn't this a monstrous joke? Lenin—a *typical* intellectual? But this does not
seem enough for Gorky. According to him, Lenin "possessed
in the highest degree the quality so characteristic for the elite
of Russian intelligentsia: self-denial which sometimes led to
self-torment, to self-mutilation. . . ." Just listen to this! The
fat is in the fire! A few pages before Gorky expatiates profusely on the subject of Lenin's heroism and that "modest asceticism with which one meets not rarely in Russia among the
honest revolutionary intellectuals who sincerely believe in the
possibility of justice on earth," and so on, and so forth. This
phrase is so disgustingly false that it is physically impossible
to go on quoting it. "Honest Russian intellectual who believes
in justice on earth." Whichever way you look at this, you can
only imagine a petty radical official from the provinces who
had gulped down the historical letters of Lavrov[3] or their
counterfeit version produced belatedly by Chernov.

This reminds me of one of those translators of Marx who
once described him in print as "the great Jeremiah of popular
affliction." Twenty-five years ago, in the small town of Nizh-
nyi Ilinsk, I laughed heartily at this Karl Marx of the provinces. And now it comes to pass that Lenin too does not escape a similar fate. It was none other than Gorky, who had
seen Lenin, who knew him well—he was among his friends—
who sometimes worked with him—this same Gorky now presents this giant of revolutionary thought not only as a pious

---

[3] *Translator's note:* P. L. Lavrov (1823–1900) mathematician, philosopher, and revolutionary writer. Took part in the Paris Commune, was a
friend of Marx and Engels. His *Historical Letters,* a philosophical work,
published in book form under the pseudonym P. Mirtov, had a tremendous
influence on Russian intelligentsia. Was one of the main ideologues of the
Populists.

ascetic, but even worse, as a typical Russian intellectual. This really borders on calumny, all the more detestable as it is made in good faith, with good intentions, and almost with enthusiasm. Of course, Vladimir Ilyich was steeped in the tradition of the radical revolutionary intelligentsia, but he transcended this tradition and only then became—Lenin. A "typical" Russian intellectual is extremely limited in his outlook; Lenin's outlook and intellect knew no limits.

If it be true to say that Lenin was nurtured by the century-old tradition of Russian radical intelligentsia, it is even more true that he was the product of the elemental force and pressure which the peasant mass has for long centuries exercised on the country. In Lenin there lived the Russian *muzhik,* with his hatred for the landlord, with his calculating spirit, his clever husbandry and his shrewdness. But Lenin transcended all that was petty and narrow in the *muzhik* by the soaring flight of his thought and his most powerful will. Finally, Lenin became the embodiment—and this was stronger in him than anything else—of the spirit of the young Russian proletariat; and not to see this, but to see only the intellectual in him, is to see nothing. What constituted Lenin's genius? It consisted precisely in this: that through him the young Russian proletariat liberated itself from the conditions shackling its development and reached toward the heights of historic universality. Lenin's personality, deeply rooted in the soil of Russia, burst forth, grew organically, expanded into creative and genuine internationalism. Lenin's genius consisted, first of all, in transcending all confines.

Gorky defines rather neatly one of Lenin's main characteristics by calling it "fighting optimism." He also adds: "In this there was nothing Russian . . ."

Well, how is it then? "The typical intellectual," the provincial "ascetic"—was not all this most Russian? Wouldn't that make, say, a good chap from Tambov? How is it then that with all these non-Russian features like an iron will and a fighting optimism, Lenin was at the same time the "typical Russian intellectual"? Isn't Gorky casting a grave aspersion on Russians generally? The talent to lead lice on a leash is unquestionably Russian, but thanks to dialectics it is not everlasting and immutable. The Social Revolutionary policy, which reached its apogee in the Kerensky regime, was the highest expression of this folklore art of leading lice on a leash. But, let me tell you, Alexei Maximovich, that the October Revolution would have been impossible if well before that date a new fire had not been kindled in Russian men and women.

Ours was the epoch not only of Russian history's turning point, but also that at which the whole national spirit underwent a transformation. You maintained, Alexei Maximovich, that Lenin's essential features were not "Russian" . . . Allow me to ask you: Is the Bolshevik Party a Russian phenomenon or perhaps . . . a Dutch phenomenon? What would you say about those proletarians engaged in clandestine work, about the fighters and partisans, about the men from the Urals, hard as rock itself, about the Red Commissars who day and night kept their fingers on the triggers of their revolvers, who today are at the head of industry, of plants and factories, and who tomorrow would be ready to lay down their lives for the liberation of the Chinese coolies? What breed of people, what species, what segment of humanity are they? Were they not made of Russian clay?

The Russia of the twentieth century (and of the earlier one as well) is no longer the old provincial land of past epochs. It is a new, an internationalist Russia with steel in its character. The Bolshevik Party is the best part of that new Russia, and Lenin its supreme builder and guide.

Here we are stepping into the thick of a great confusion. Gorky declares himself, not without belated coquetry, "a doubting Marxist" who does not believe in the intelligence of the masses in general and the intelligence of the peasantry in particular. He maintains that the masses have to be ruled "from outside," from above.

"I know," Gorky goes on, "that by voicing such ideas I am exposing myself again to the scorn of politicians. I also know that the most intelligent and the most honest among them will mock me insincerely, from their so-called sense of duty."

I do not know who those "intelligent" and "honest" politicians are who share Gorky's skepticism about the masses. But their skepticism seems to me rather flat. That the masses need guidance ("from outside"), that much, we think, Lenin had guessed. Perhaps Gorky has heard that precisely because of that need Lenin spent his whole conscious life in building up a special organization, namely the Bolshevik Party. Lenin never encouraged any blind faith in the reason of the masses, but he had even more contempt for the arrogance and conceit of the intellectual who reproached the masses that they were not made in his excellent image and after his likeness. Lenin was aware that the intelligence of the masses had to be adapted to the objective development of circumstances. The party was to facilitate this process. History testifies that it achieved its task.

Gorky, as he says himself, parted with the Communists because of a divergence of views on the role of the intellectuals. He maintains that the better ones among the old Bolsheviks brought up hundreds of workers precisely "in the spirit of social heroism and high intellectuality." (!!) In simpler words and more exactly it means that Gorky accepted Bolshevism in its laboratory stage, when it was forming and educating its first intellectual and working class cadres. He feels near enough to the Bolshevik of 1903–1905. But the man of 1917, mature and formed, who with a sure hand put into practice what fifteen years before one could only perceive—such a Bolshevik is a stranger whom Gorky views with hostility.

Gorky himself, with his constant aspirations toward higher

culture and higher intelligence, managed somehow to stop halfway. He is neither a layman nor a Pope of culture, but some sort of a psalmist. Hence his haughty attitude, his contempt for the intelligence of the masses and also for Marxism, though Marxism, in contrast with subjectivism, bases itself not on faith in the reason of the masses, but on the logic of the materialistic processes which, in the final analysis, determine and form that "reason."

But that road is not easy and on the way quite a lot of crockery gets broken (some of it created by "culture"). This is what Gorky cannot endure. According to him, one should be satisfied with just admiring all these lovely ceramics, all the pottery, the pots and pans; one should not break them.

Gorky wants to find an affinity with Lenin, and so he consoles himself thus: "Vladimir Ilyich also, probably more than once, had to hold down his soul by its wings," that means to do violence to himself: Implacable when he had to crush resistance, Lenin was thus a prey to interior conflicts because he had to restrain his love of man, his love of culture. In such a way Gorky presents Lenin as the heir to the respectable malaise, the "sick conscience," that split personality, which once upon a time was the bane of the old radical intelligentsia. But all this is untrue. Lenin was all of a piece: "a piece" of very high quality, of complex structure, but with all its components held perfectly together and constituting one solid entity.

The truth is that Lenin often avoided busybodies, mediators, and petitioners. "Let X talk to him," he used to say with an evasive smile, "I may prove too good." Yes, he sometimes feared to prove "too good," because he knew the craftiness of the foe and the sanctimonious foolishness of mediators and considered in advance that no amount of caution was too much. He preferred to deal with the invisible enemy rather than be distracted by accidental circumstances where he might show himself "too good." But even in this there was his calm political calculation and by no means that "sickly conscience" which always goes together with lack of will, lachrymosity, and the maudlin nature of the "typical Russian intellectual."

But this is not yet all. Gorky, as he himself tells us, reproached Lenin with a "simplified understanding of the drama of existence" (hm, hm!); such poor understanding, he says, "puts culture in mortal danger" (hm, hm!). During the critical days at the end of 1917 and the beginning of 1918, when in Moscow shots were fired at the Kremlin, when sailors were throwing cigarette butts at the Gobelins (such things did happen, but not as often as the bourgeoisie alleged), when soldiers, as it was said, were cutting up the canvases of Rembrandt to make themselves trousers (extremely uncomfortable and not very practical)—this was the kind of complaint with which whimpering representatives of "high intellectuality" were coming to Gorky. At that time Gorky quite lost his balance and became a real mourner of culture. Horror and vandalism! The Bolsheviks are going to break all the historical vases and pots, flower pots, kitchen pots, and chamber pots!

And Lenin would answer: "We shall break as many as we have to, and if we break too many, the fault will lie not with us but with those intellectuals who defend untenable positions." Wasn't this proof of a narrow mind? Don't you see— Oh, Lord, have mercy—that Lenin oversimplified "the drama of existence"?

It is not worth while even to quibble about all this. Lenin's whole life was devoted not to bemoaning the complexity of existence, but to changing it. For this, existence has to be viewed in its entirety, with its main elements and trends of further development clearly seen; all else is of little significance. Precisely because Lenin had this great talent of creatively going straight into the heart of the matter, he considered "the drama of existence" in a businesslike manner: We shall break this, we have to demolish that, and temporarily we have to prop up something else.

Lenin noted all that was honest, all that was individual. He noticed all particulars and every detail. If he "simplified" or, in other words, rejected all that was unessential, it was not because he did not see it, but because he knew to perfection the relative value and proportion of things.

All this brings to my mind a worker by the name of Vorontsov, who just after October was detailed to guard Lenin's person and to help him. As we were preparing to evacuate Petrograd, Vorontsov said to me gravely, "If it so happens that *they* take Petrograd, *they* might find quite a lot that's useful . . . We should put dynamite under the whole city and blow it all up."

"Wouldn't you regret the loss of Petrograd, Comrade Vorontsov?" I asked, admiring his boldness.

"What is there to be regretted? When we are back, we shall build something much better."

I have not invented that brief dialogue, nor have I stylized it. Such as it was, it remained engraved on my memory. That was the correct attitude toward culture. No lamentation and no wails of woe. Culture is the product of human hands. True culture lies not in the decorated pots of history, but in the good organization of the labor of human hands and minds. If on the way to achieve such an organization there are obstacles, they have to be swept aside. And if, in the process, we are forced to destroy some values of the past, then let us destroy them, but without sentimental tears. We shall return to build anew and to build incomparably better. That was how Lenin, and with him millions of men and women, felt and thought. This was right and just. From this revolutionaries of all countries can learn a great deal.

Kislovodsk
September 28, 1924

4. Children on Lenin[1]

*In Russia
There was only one
Vladimir Ilyich Lenin.*
—From a child's poem

A delightful and quite exceptional little book has appeared recently: a collection of children's writings about the life and death of Lenin.[2] The authors, whose ages range between nine and fourteen years—there is even one girl of five—write about the great old man.

Of course, many simply reproduce what they had heard from the grown-ups. But here and there among the stereotyped texts appears an unexpected breath of such freshness that the most familiar phrases come to life again, as if revived by a spring shower; one also finds the inimitable, colorful spontaneity of creative childhood. The poems are, as usual, rather weaker than the prose. Rules of poetry writing are too restrictive and hamper directness of expression. But even among the poems some are astonishing.

"There is no such spot," writes one child, "where they would not know the father of the proletariat, the strong, the courageous, the brave, the resourceful, the wise Lenin." This list, in which the finest qualities are enumerated one after the other, completely expresses the children's ideas about Lenin:

---

[1] *Translator's note:* This essay is not included in the first Russian edition of Trotsky's book. Here it is translated from *Pravda*, October 8, 1924.

[2] *Ilyich,* ed. Anna Grinberg, *Novaya Moskva,* 1924.

He possesses all the virtues that make a man absolutely perfect.

"When he was imprisoned with his comrades, he always sang: 'Forward, comrades, forward!' " This remark shows a deep conviction that in prison one should not become dejected, one should keep up the spirit of one's mates, and so "the brave, resourceful" Vladimir Ilyich goes on singing "Forward, comrades, forward." The others sing with him, but, of course, he leads the chorus. Who else could lead it? The same child continues: "Before, when Lenin was still alive, I was sure that if nothing came of the German revolution and if the capitalist countries marched on Russia, then Ilyich, although already ill, would get up from his bed and would fight to the last drop of blood. That was how I imagined Ilyich would sacrifice himself." One can see here how political ideas, drawn from newspaper articles (the defeat of the German revolution, capitalist attack on the Soviet Union) are linked with the direct, spontaneous yet convincing and unspoiled childish images: When the revolution is in trouble, the ill and aged Ilyich rises from his bed and fights "to the last drop of his blood." Only death prevented him from "sacrificing himself" on the final barricade. The author ends his piece thus: "Now that Lenin is no more one should not be afraid." Once this boy grows up, he will surely find a place for himself on the Leninist barricades.

There is also in the book a biography of Lenin in which the whole story of Lenin's family is told. We learn about his father, about Alexander who was shot, and about his sister Maria, now the "editress" of *Pravda*. Exiled to Siberia, Lenin liked "playing games and often went racing on skates or something else, and when he ran he would strain all his forces to win the race and not to be beaten by the others." As you see, this image of Lenin is quite different from that so often presented to us: Lenin, the morose saint, who wherever he appears looks immediately for a dark humid room where he can shut himself up. What disgusting bigotry! No, the children's Lenin—and the real one—liked running races and "strained all his forces so as not to be beaten by others."

I cannot refrain from recalling an amusing episode. Together with Vladimir Ilyich we introduced a "rule" that anybody coming more than ten minutes late to a session should pay a fine. I remember that just after emerging from one meeting we had to attend another taking place at the far end of the Kremlin, for which we had to cross a very long esplanade. Ilyich decided to go home for a while. I phoned him. "Vladimir Ilyich, you risk paying a fine, you have only two to three minutes left before the session begins."

"It's all right," answered Ilyich with a little giggle, the sense of which I understood only later. I walked downstairs, and, reaching the courtyard, I kept on looking back to see whether Vladimir Ilyich was anywhere to be seen. Suddenly, at the far end, about a hundred paces in front of me, a familiar figure whizzed past and vanished round the corner of the Cavalry Building. "Was this Lenin? Impossible. It cannot be."

Two minutes later I reached the conference room. Whom did I see? Lenin. Still slightly short of breath, he met me with a joyful "Hello, it is you who are one minute late!" and he burst out in triumphant laughter.

"I must admit," I explained to the other comrades, "I did not expect . . . True, it seemed to me that someone resembling Vladimir Ilyich flew by toward the Cavalry Building, but I could not imagine that the Chairman of the Council of People's Commissars would—in the full view of all—rush like a hurricane across the esplanade of the Kremlin." Ilyich was chuckling; he was triumphant. All this happened exactly as in that child's biography: Vladimir Ilyich summoned all his strength and would not let anybody overtake him.

But let us go back to the main story.

After the Siberian exile—emigration; after that—the revolution, and then the man had to go into hiding to avoid being caught by Kerensky. The children forget nothing. "Even from his hiding place Comrade Lenin was directing the revolution and was sending out letters. And when the Soviet was in session, Lenin *presided over it from his hut* as a delegate present at the meeting." Could this have been put better? Here is Lenin hidden in a shack and, as Chairman, presiding over the assembly of the national deputies. This was indeed how things happened. However, the vagaries of the climate made such a method of governing rather inconvenient. "It started raining," the young biographer goes on, "and it became cold in the hut." The tactic had to be modified and some other way of directing the revolution had to be found. Of course, Ilyich found it; not for nothing was he "strong, courageous, brave, resourceful, wise." He went for a time to Finland. And this is what later happened: "Comrade Ilyich had no more patience to wait; he returned to Piter [Petersburg] and there organized the October insurrection. Power was taken over by workers and peasants." This was true. It is even true that Lenin had "no more patience to wait."

One of the young authors describes his meeting with Lenin. The boy was with his father in the Kremlin, on the esplanade. Suddenly Ilyich, after shaking hands with the father, stretched his hand toward the boy. "I got so excited that I dropped my basket. Before I had time to pick it up, Vladimir Ilyich had already bent down and then he shook my hand which I put out to take the basket from him. Then he put his hand on my head and asked my father, 'Is it this one or your older one who is a Bolshevik?'

" 'This one. The older one is a White Guardist. He fights against the young scamps of Comrade Trotsky, and he is also too lazy to learn . . .'

" 'Well, never mind! The time will come when he will also be a Bolshevik,' says Vladimir Ilyich.

"He spoke quickly and smiled all the time."

This dialogue is reproduced with admirable exactitude: the

words, the turn of phrase, and the gestures were really Lenin's. Indeed, "He spoke quickly and smiled all the time." This faithfulness in reproduction of the conversation is due to the receptiveness and freshness of memory of the author. To listen to Lenin was to him like the first sight of a tremendous fire or a tremendous waterfall.

Another little boy listened to Lenin who spoke at the Red Square to the workers, urging them to unite and form one big family. "I stood in the car next to the driver and I looked at Lenin. *I liked him.*" The author does not bother to explain why. For him it is absolutely clear that people are divided into those that one likes and those one does not. *"I liked him."* That is all. Full stop.

Yet another boy describes how he saw Lenin. He had a more difficult job. "On the square there was an enormous crowd and everybody shouted 'Ilyich.' I wanted to climb onto something, but there was nothing. I was pushed about. I even started to cry because I so much wanted to see Lenin. In the end I grabbed the back of a workman, I put my foot into his pocket, and then I hoisted myself onto his shoulder as if on horseback. I thought he would shake me off straightway and give me a kick too. To my surprise the workman, saying that I was a rascal, told me to hold fast to his neck. I found myself two heads above everybody else and I saw Ilyich."

Well, you will admit that not everybody would find a similar way. In any case, you would probably be put off by the mere idea of *your* foot in a *stranger's* pocket. But our Alexander of Macedon from the Presnia suburb is not put off by such a trifle. And because it had occurred to him to put *his* foot into the pocket of a stranger and because in addition the stranger did not slap him, but allowed him to remain on his observation post (not, however, without calling him a rascal), we have received a remarkable eyewitness description of Lenin as speaker.

"He got up on the platform. He was wearing a dark, I think

a black suit, a shirt with a turn-down collar and a tie, and a cap on his head. He pulled a white handkerchief from his pocket and wiped his bald head. I do not remember what he said. I was really paying more attention to how he was speaking. *Sometimes he kept bending down quite low from the platform,* stretching his arms in front of him; he had his handkerchief in his hand and often wiped his forehead. He often smiled. I was watching his face, his nose, his lips, and his small beard. His speech was often interrupted by clapping and shouting. And so I also shouted."

Indeed, how could one refrain from shouting? What exemplary precision in the portrayal. Lenin wipes his forehead and his bald head with a white handkerchief, now and again bends down stretching his arms toward the crowd. How alive Lenin is in this picture. What he actually said, our author does not remember. This does not really matter, as the speech anyhow was taken down by stenographers. The lively figure of Lenin, however, remains engraved on the eager memory of a little man sitting on a stranger's back. "I was watching his face, his nose, his lips, and his small beard"—he will remember this all his life. On his way home he kept on repeating: Lenin, Lenin, Lenin. The boy was carrying away a host of wonderful impressions. He stopped to look at every photograph of Lenin on the street . . . Lenin died without knowing that sometimes in order to watch him one had to put one's foot in a stranger's pocket. How wholeheartedly he would have laughed at this "Bolshevik" manner of solving a difficult tactical problem . . .

Here is another detail from the biography of the leader:

"Lenin liked fishing. On a hot day he would take his fishing rod and would sit down on the bank of a river and *all the time he would think how to improve the life of the workers and peasants.*" What imagination! The hook is thrown into the water; the man sits on the bank and waits until the fish takes the bait (which does not happen often); in the meantime he looks at the water and thinks hard, very hard, how to improve the lot of workers and peasants. That's what Lenin did! And because of this the fishing is seen in a meaningful light:

> There was only one
> Vladimir Ilyich Lenin. . . .

In races he ran fast; he did not like the czar and the capitalists; he was fishing and thinking hard how to improve the life of workers and peasants. In prison he was singing aloud "Forward, comrades, forward"; he directed the revolution from a hut and was loudly urging the workers to unite and was wiping his bald head with a handkerchief; he knew everything, he was wise, and he taught. But he died. The strong and courageous father of the proletariat died. And this extraordinary, mysterious, and terrible news which came from above, from the grown-ups, shattered the children's world.

On January 22 the teacher at school was speaking about Lenin's death. "And the teacher, much affected, talked haltingly and we, all of us, listened intently and in the end we could not stand it any longer and hot tears were flowing down our cheeks. Then the children could not listen any more, because they were all crying and so we all got up and sang the Funeral March."

The boys and girls who on January 22, 1924, were shedding hot tears and singing the Funeral March will relate all this to their children and their grandchildren. And so the story will be passed on from generation to generation.

The news of Lenin's death reaches a worker's family: "My mother sat at the table and had a knife in her hand. When she heard about the death of Ilyich, she dropped the knife and she started to cry although she did not know her great leader." How convincing is the "dropped knife" and how well the child remarks that the mother cried *"although she did not know her great leader."*

A little girl returned home after having listened to a talk on Lenin, and she "related every detail to her family: that Ilyich did not like luxuries, that he liked children, that he liked to work a lot." Everything has its place: the work is put last and "luxuries" first, children just in the middle. An adult would probably see things in a different order. It was only after hearing the girl's story that the mother gave credence to the news and "got very alarmed." Then the girl together with her Komsomol sister sat down to sew black ties.

A small boy from a Children's Home relates how Oscar Andreevich (evidently quite familiar to the author, though unknown to us) was draping a black flag as a sign of mourning. "And there goes a fat woman and pushing us aside she says: 'Out of the way. . . . Haven't you seen how rags are being put out?' And I said *very, very quietly,* 'Stupid woman, she doesn't understand a thing!' " John Huss remarked of an old ignorant woman, "Oh, holy simplicity!"—different formula, different epoch, and different the age of the man who pronounced the words, but the spirit was the same.

"At the beginning of that day we were cheerful, but when we learned—we became very sad." How expressive is this brevity. Then they go to see the dead. "The coffin, a red cushion. He was there, very pale. I looked at him all the time." The little John Huss woke up next morning, and he very much wanted to have a portrait of Lenin. That is what he says. "In the morning I got up and *I greatly needed* Lenin's portrait." Straightway he drew a picture and to give vent to his feelings, he placed a small red star and the letters USSR and RSFSR on Lenin's forehead. In this way everybody would know whose picture it was.

"Dear great leader," writes a little girl to the dead Lenin, "I thought that you will recover, but unexpectedly death came. I so much regret it and it makes me so sad that I shall not see you any more." With these words she ends her brief letter which will be read by everyone except its addressee.

"Echoes in the hills resound:
Ilyich is no more
But an answer can be found:
Do not lose courage."

Well, the rhymes are rather poor, but how much they express: the death of Ilyich has moved even the hills and the author hears the echo in Moscow. However, this somber news must be met by a call for bravery and courage. It was not in vain that Lenin taught his comrades in prison to sing: "Forward, comrades, forward."

Lenin is dead. He is carried to the House of the Trade Unions in Moscow where his body is laid out.

"They looked at him, the young and the old,
The peasant and the worker—and yet *he did not know.*
Once he gave us the Soviets.
Now he lay in his coffin
Quite still."

"And yet he did not know . . ." The author became suddenly aware that Lenin who knew everything, yet now did not know that people looked at him. Such is the meaning of death.

And now the funeral. "Around the House of the Trade Unions many people were waiting for him. The citizens of the town did not expect to meet him in such a manner. They thought, Here will come the chief ruler in a golden carriage and all will be glittering. But the workers recognized in him their own, their well-beloved Ilyich." On the one hand a political distinction between the "citizens of the town" and the worker; on the other, the truly childish images—"the chief ruler," "the golden carriage," all "glittering."

Another description of the funeral:

"One speaker, and another, and the third, and the fourth,
From different countries, from different states they came.
Now the last words are already said
And *Lenin without fear* descends into the tomb."

The small heart is rent at the idea that Ilyich, that Lenin
has to descend into the grave, but here comes a clear and
consoling thought: ". . . without fear . . ." How could it
be otherwise: Fearless all his life and now he died without
fear. This is no mysticism, but an artistic image of the leader.

Endlessly, endlessly, people are passing in front of the red
coffin, adults and children—the future authors of reminiscences:

"And behind us I could hear somebody sobbing,
Somebody's piercing scream.
We are passing and passing with our hearts throbbing,
Seeing his yellowing face never enough seen."

This is well said; especially good is the last line.

Here is another story, realistically descriptive, less lyrical,
and without political accents.

"We joined one of the queues on Mokhovaya Street. In
front of us we could see only heads, and heads, and above
them banners. The crowd was silent. Then a peddler passes and
shouts: 'Hot pies, hot pies.' A woman said: 'Go away, this is
no time for pies!' The queue moves slowly and there are already many people behind us. Everybody feels the cold. The
frost pinches our feet, our hands, and faces." Did Shakespeare
learn from children the gift of combining the tragic with
the trivial, the great with the petty? Under a bleak sky millions of people are burying their leader. Amid all this: "Hot
pies, hot pies!" and the rebuff: "Go away, this is no time for
pies." Finally, our author reached the hall: "On a raised platform the red coffin and he in the coffin. One would give one's
life to save him. No, that is impossible. The illness took what

belonged to it. His face is yellowish, as if made of wax. The nose sharper, the expression severe. The beard exactly as in pictures, and the arms in repose as if he were alive. He is dressed in a green French[3] and on his breast the Order of the Red Banner." How observant the eye of the author and with what precision he conveys his impressions. Through the sober, factual description bursts out the sentiment in all its freshness: "One would give one's life to save him." A little further the narrative is again interrupted by an exclamation: "Oh, too soon, Ilyich, too soon." This sounds like a reproach, but it comes from the bottom of the heart. The most cogent remark ends the piece:

"People descend and go out, but their faces are not as they were before: waiting to be let into the hall, they were expectant and a little impatient; now, with their heads bent, they all look down—everybody tries to fix the image of Vladimir Ilyich in their memory forever."

This essay shows such power of observation and is so well done that one might suspect an adult had written it. And yet an adult would not write in this manner; I, at least, have not come across anything like it.

"He was lying in the red coffin," writes a very young author (or rather authoress—a *pendant* to the "editress"), "and there was music and his beard was just the same as it used to be in his pictures. When I saw this, I started crying."

No, one could not hold back the tears when one saw the beard, the same beard which he had when he was alive. In children's recollections Lenin's beard becomes a very important element. It seems to symbolize maturity, manliness, and the fighting spirit. Lenin had a small beard, but it was full of meaning because it was *his*. Also the beard was "exactly like in the pictures," the pictures were therefore true; therefore everything else was true. The little girl goes on to describe

[3] *Translator's note:* A kind of military jacket common in Russia since the war.

how all by herself she made a badge to pin onto her frock.
The quotation would take us too far. But anyone seriously
thinking of producing a Lenin badge with no money to buy
one, should read this book. He will find in it all the required
information . . .

One more poem, a dramatic one, about the death of Lenin:

> "When they were carrying you to the grave
> Millions of people were walking behind you,
> They were walking with flags and banners.
> People were crying, cannons were firing,
> Factory sirens were whining.
> *The whole world knew that you were dead.*"

This was how we buried the leader. The plants and the factories were shaken by the sound of sirens and cannons. The
flags and the banners and the cannons proclaimed the greatness of the deceased. Millions were crying over your grave.
"The whole world knew . . ." Thus we were burying you,
Ilyich. Thus we were parting from you.

Perhaps the best is the funeral dirge sung by a five-year-old
girl in a kindergarten:

> "You died, Ilyich.
> A bird flew in
> And warmed itself in the sun.
> You died, Ilyich!
> And you were buried.
> And your clothes died.
> You died, Ilyich!
> And you were left all alone,
> Poor, poor Ilyich.
> You were good.
> I shall give you my room
> And I love you.
> You'll come back into the light again
> And we shall be able to touch you."

The little girl's thoughts are wandering: It is so difficult to concentrate and to collect one's thoughts. A bird flies in and warms itself. But something grave has happened: Ilyich died and was buried and his clothes died with him, because they live and die. "You were left all alone, poor, poor Ilyich!" But is all this so final? Perhaps if I give you my room you will return into the light again and we shall be able to touch you. Does not life mean that one can touch and be touched? This was what a little girl sang about Lenin. Nobody has composed a better song. Great poets will come much later; they will read what the children wrote in this book; they will ponder deeply, and they will sing:

> In Russia
> There was only one
> Vladimir Ilyich Lenin.

Kislovodsk
September 30, 1924

5. Lenin Wounded [1]

Comrades, the brotherly greetings with which I am received are for me a sign that in these difficult hours and days all of us, like brothers, feel a profound need to draw closer to each other, to our Soviet institutions, to tighten our ranks under the Communist banner. In these hours and days of anxiety when the standard-bearer of our proletariat, and, we can say, of the world proletariat, is struggling with the terrible specter of death, we feel closer to each other than in the hours of victory . . .

[1] Speech at the session of the All-Union Central Executive Committee, September 2, 1918.

The news of the attempt at Lenin's life reached me and some other comrades in Svyazhsk, on the Kazan front. Blows were falling fast, from the right, from the left, and from the front. But this latest blow hit us at the back; it was delivered from behind. Treachery opened up another front, the most painful, and at the present time the most alarming: the one on which Vladimir Ilyich struggles against death.

I firmly believe together with all of you, that from all the battles we might still have to fight, we shall soon emerge victorious. Whatever partial defeats we may still suffer, none will be as terrible, as tragic for the working class of Russia and of the whole world, as the fatal issue of the battle going on for the life of our leader.

One can imagine quite easily with what violent hatred all the enemies of the working class look upon Lenin and will be looking upon him. It is as if nature were producing its very best by embodying in one man both the essence of revolutionary thought and the indomitable energy of the proletariat. Such a man is Vladimir Ilyich.

The gallery of those who led the revolutionary fighters is rich and varied. Like other comrades who have been engaged in revolutionary work for nearly three decades, I have met in many countries various types of workers' leaders, of revolutionary representatives of the working class. But only Comrade Lenin is the man truly created for our epoch of blood and iron.

We have left behind the period of the so-called peaceful development of bourgeois society, when conflicts of interests were only gradually mounting, when Europe was experiencing a time of what was called armed peace, and blood was flowing only in the colonies where rapacious capital was tormenting the most backward peoples. Europe enjoyed peace under the regime of capitalist militarism. It was also the formative period for the most notable leaders of the European labor movement who then were coming to the fore. Among them was the

great and brilliant August Bebel. But in him was mirrored
the epoch of the gradual and slow development of the working class; he combined great courage and iron energy with
extreme prudence in action; he kept probing the situation and
his was the strategy of waiting and preparation. He expressed
the process of gradual, molecular gathering of forces; his
thought proceeded step by step in the same manner in which
the German working class in the period of reaction was itself
moving forward step by step, freeing itself from obscurantism
and prejudice. His moral stature grew, expanded, acquired
strength and magnitude, but always on the same basis of waiting and preparation. Such were the ideas and the methods of
August Bebel, the most valuable figure of that epoch which
has already passed into the eternity of history.

Ours is a different epoch—the time when old accumulated
contradictions reached an explosive stage, breaking through
the surface of bourgeois society when the very foundations of
world capitalism were shaken by the terrible slaughter of European nations. In our epoch all the various class antagonisms
were laid bare and the masses were forced to face the horrible
reality of the death of millions for the sake of the profit and
riches of a handful. And for such an epoch Western Europe
forgot, or was unable, to provide a leader. This was not just
an accident: all leaders who on the eve of war enjoyed the
greatest trust of the European working class represented the
yesterdays of that class and not the actuality of the present
day . . .

When the new epoch dawned, the old chiefs were unable
to keep pace with that age of terrible convulsions and bloody
battles. History wished, not fortuitously, to create in Russia a
figure carved in rock, a figure which accorded well with all
the ferocity and greatness of the times. No, it was no accident.

The year 1847 produced in backward Germany the figure
of Karl Marx, the greatest fighter and thinker that ever charted
history's new roads. Yes, Germany was then a backward

country, but at the same time Germany's intelligentsia was going through a phase of revolutionary development; its most eminent representative, enriched by all the science it had acquired, broke with bourgeois society, and choosing the side of revolutionary proletariat, elaborated a program for the labor movement and for the working class a theory of its development.

What Marx had predicted in his time, our epoch has been called upon to fulfill. For this new leaders were needed, leaders who would carry in them the flame of the new age in which the working class, having risen to the height of its historic task, clearly saw the great divide that had to be crossed if mankind was to be saved, if it was not to be allowed to putrefy like carrion dropped by the roadside of history.

For this new age Russian history created a new leader.

All that was best in the old revolutionary intellectuals of earlier times—their spirit of self-denial, their audacity, their hatred of oppression—all this was concentrated in the figure of this man who, already in his youth, broke irrevocably with the intelligentsia because it was too strongly tied to the bourgeoisie; this man absorbed completely the spirit and the just cause of the working class. Supported by Russia's young revolutionary proletariat, utilizing the rich experience of a worldwide workers' movement, transforming its ideology into a lever for action, he has risen to his full stature on the political horizon. This is Lenin, the greatest man of our revolutionary epoch. [Applause]

I know, and you know as well as I do, comrades, that the fate of the working class does not depend on individual personalities; but this does not mean that the individual personality is of no importance in the development of the working class. The individual cannot remold the working class after his own image and likeness, nor can he, at will, show the proletariat this or that road to follow, but he can help in the accomplishment of the necessary tasks and speed up the attainment of the goal. Critics reproached Karl Marx that he expected the revolution to come about much sooner than in reality it took place. The answer, and a very valid one, to this reproach was that Marx stood on the top of a high mountain and from there the distance seemed to him much shorter than it was.

Vladimir Ilyich was often criticized by many comrades, myself among them, for seemingly not paying attention to secondary matters and certain side issues. I should think that in times of "normal" slow development this might have been a defect in a political leader; but in this lay Comrade Lenin's preeminence as the leader of a new epoch, in which all that is unessential, all that is incidental and secondary recedes into the background, becomes overshadowed, and what remains is only the basic irreconcilable class antagonism in the acute form of civil war. It was Lenin's peculiar gift, which he possessed to the highest degree, that with his intense revolutionary gaze, he could see and point out to others what was most important, most necessary, and most essential. Those comrades who, like myself, were given the chance to observe Lenin's activity and the working of his mind at close quarters, could not help but enthusiastically admire—yes, I repeat, enthusiastically admire—the perspicacity, the acuteness of his thought which rejected all that was external, accidental, superficial, and reached to the heart of the matter and grasped the essential methods of action. The working class learns to value only those leaders who, having opened new paths, go forward with determination even if the proletariat's own prejudices temporarily hinder their progress.

To Lenin's powerful thought is added the power of his will; such thought and such will go into the making of a truly revolutionary leader, courageous, strong in mind, and unshaken in determination.

It is our good fortune that in all we say and hear and read in resolutions about Lenin we do not bemoan his loss. And

yet we were so near this . . . We are sure that in the battle
which goes on in the Kremlin, life will overcome and that
Vladimir Ilyich will soon return to our ranks.

Comrades, I said that Lenin is the embodiment of the
courageous thought and revolutionary will of the proletariat.
There seems to be a symbol, an intentional pattern of history
in the fact that in these difficult hours when the Russian proletariat, straining all forces, fights on the military fronts
against the Czechoslovaks, the White Guards, the mercenaries of England and France, our leader struggles with the
wounds inflicted on him by the agents of the same White
Guards, the same Czechoslovaks, and the same Anglo-French
mercenaries. There is here an inner bond and a profound historical symbol. Just as we are all convinced that in this our
fight on the Czechoslovak, Anglo-French and White-Guardist
front we grow stronger with every day, with every hour that
passes [applause]—and I speak here as an eyewitness who has
returned straight from the scene of military operations—yes,
we are growing in strength and we shall be stronger tomorrow
than we have been today, and the day after we shall be even
stronger—I do not doubt that soon the time will come when
we shall be able to tell you that Kazan and Simbirsk, Samara
and Ufa, and other towns temporarily occupied by the enemy,
are rejoining our Soviet family—in the same way, we firmly
hope we shall see the speedy recovery of Comrade Lenin. But
even now, at this very moment, the splendid image of our
wounded leader, who is out of action for the time being, stands
clearly before us. We know that he has never left our ranks,
because even when mowed down by treacherous bullets, he
prods us all to action, he rouses us and urges us to move forward. I have not seen a single comrade, a single honest worker
who would, on learning the news about the base attempt on
Lenin's life, let his arms fall in dejection. On the contrary, I
saw dozens who clenched their fists, whose hands sought their

guns; I saw and I heard hundreds who vowed implacable vengeance on the class enemies of the proletariat.

There is no need to relate to you what were the feelings of the fighters on the front when they learned that Lenin was lying here with two bullets in his body. Nobody could ever say that there was no steel in Lenin's character; now the enemy drove steel right into his flesh. This makes him even more precious to the working class of Russia.

I do not know whether our words and the throbbing of our hearts can be heard at Lenin's bedside, but I have no doubt that he feels it all. I have no doubt that even through his fever he feels that our hearts beat two and three times stronger. Clearer than ever before we are now aware that we are all members of one Soviet Communist family. Never yet has the life of any one of us seemed to us so secondary in importance as it does now, at a moment when the life of the greatest man of our times is in mortal peril. Any imbecile can fire at Lenin's head, but to create such a head is a hard task even for nature itself.

Yes, yes, he will soon be up again to think, to build, to fight together with us. On our part we promise our dear leader that as long as there still exists some power of thought and hot blood still throbs in our hearts, we shall remain faithful to the banner of the Communist revolution. Against the enemies of the working class we shall fight to our last breath, to our last drop of blood. [Stormy and prolonged applause]

6. *Lenin Ill* [1]

Comrades, during the year our party has been subjected to a new test, in its capacity for clear thinking and in the firm-

[1] From a speech at the seventh conference of the Ukrainian Communist Party, April 5, 1923.

ness of its will. This test was all the more severe because it came as a consequence of an event which weighs heavily on the consciousness of all members of the party, of the broad masses of the working population, or, to be more accurate, on the working masses of our country and, to a considerable degree, on the working masses of the whole world. I am speaking of the illness of Vladimir Ilyich. At the beginning of March his condition took a turn for the worse and the Politbureau met in session to consider ways of informing the party and the country about the deterioration of his state. You will, I am sure, all realize the mood of the session, at which we had to issue to the public this first sad and alarming bulletin.

Of course, even in such a moment we had to bear in mind our political responsibilities. Nobody will reproach us with this. We had to think not only of the state of health of Comrade Lenin. True, we were all preoccupied with his physical condition, with his pulse, his heart, his fever; but we also had to think about the reaction which the medical bulletin would have on the political pulse and the political heartbeat of the working class and of our party.

With anxiety, but also with profound faith in the strength of our party, we decided that our comrades and the whole country should be informed at the appearance of the first danger signal. Nobody was in doubt that our enemies would try to exploit the news in order to sow panic among the population, especially in the countryside, to spread all sorts of alarmist rumors, and so on, and so forth. Yet we were all convinced that the party should immediately know how things stood, because to tell the truth amounted to raising the sense of responsibility of each and every member of the party.

Ours is a vast organization embracing half a million people. This is a great community with a great deal of experience, and in this huge mass of comrades Lenin's place is absolutely unique. The whole of history does not know of a single man who could have had such an influence on the destiny not only of one country but on that of the whole of mankind; there is no yardstick, there can be none, to measure the historical importance of Lenin. It is therefore understandable that the fact of his prolonged absence from work and of his serious condition could not but provoke deep anxiety in our political life. Of course, of course, we know that the toiling masses will achieve victory. Don't we have in our song the words: "Nobody will become our savior . . ."; and further: not even "a hero . . ." This is true in the final reckoning of history: the working classes finally will conquer, even if there had been no Karl Marx, even if Ulyanov-Lenin had never existed. The working class would by itself have arrived at the ideas which it needed and would have elaborated the methods called for, but all this would have been much delayed, would have been much slower. The circumstance that at two high points in its development, the working class was granted two such figures as that of Marx and of Lenin proved a tremendous advantage to the revolution. Marx was a prophet with the Tables of the Law; Lenin was the executor of the Commandments, addressing himself not to the aristocracy of proletariat as Marx had done, but speaking to the masses, to the people, acquiring new experience in the most difficult conditions, acting, maneuvering, and coming out victorious.

This year Vladimir Ilyich could only partly share in our practical work. In matters of ideology we have had from him recently a few warnings and directives concerning the question of peasantry, of the state apparatus, and the problem of nationalities. These guidelines will serve us well for quite a few years.

And now we have to announce the deterioration in his physical condition. It was natural that we should ask ourselves with deep anxiety how would this news be received by those outside the party—by the Red Army man, by the peasant. In our ruling circle Lenin is the only one who had the confidence of the peasant masses. Apart from everything else, Lenin represents the great moral capital of our Soviet Government in the relations between the working class and the peasantry. Would not the peasants expect—some of us were wondering —that Lenin's policy would undergo a change since he himself was out of action for such a prolonged period? How would the party react to the news? What effect would the bulletin have on the working classes, on the country?

After the first alarming bulletins were published, the whole party pulled itself together, closed its ranks and improved its morale. Naturally, comrades, the party consists of living human beings, and human beings have their failings and weaknesses; among Communists there is a great deal of what is "human, only too human," as the German saying goes. There are among Communists factional conflicts, personal conflicts, some serious disagreements and some insignificant ones, and there always will be, because a large party cannot live otherwise. But the moral strength of the party, its political worth, is determined by what comes to the surface at the time of a tragic crisis like the present: the discipline, the wish for unity, or, on the contrary, the incidental, the personal, the "human, all too human." I think, comrades, that by now we can already with certainty draw the following conclusion: Feeling that it might for a long time be deprived of Lenin's leadership, the party has become more united than ever; it has rejected all that might endanger the clarity of its thought, the unity of its will and its fighting capacity . . .

Before I took the train to come here to Kharkov, I had talked to our Moscow Commander Nikolai Ivanovich Muralov, whom many of you know as an old Bolshevik, about the effect the news of Lenin's illness has had on the Red Army men. Muralov said: At first they were all as if struck by thunder, they instinctively recoiled, but then they reflected and began to think more seriously about Lenin and all he represented.

Yes, comrades, the non-party soldier of the Red Army began to wonder in his own way, but in all seriousness, about the role of the individual in history; he began to think about those problems which we of the older generation learned as schoolboys or students or young workers from books read in prisons, in hard labor camps or in exile where we discussed and argued about the relations between "the hero" and "the masses," about subjective and objective factors in a given situation, and so on, and so forth. And now, here, in 1923 our young soldier turned his mind toward all these problems and toward the concrete question of Lenin's role in history; and with the soldiers hundreds of thousands of Russian and Ukrainian and other peasants are posing the same question. What answer do they receive from our political instructors, from our commissars, from our group secretaries? They say: Lenin is a genius; a genius is born no more than once in a century, and world history knows only two who have assumed the leadership of the working class, and these two are Marx and Lenin. One cannot create a genius by decree of even the most powerful and most disciplined party, but one can try within the limits of one's possibilities to make up for the absent genius by redoubling our collective efforts. In such a form our political instructors can popularize the theory of relations between the individual and the class among the non-party army men. This is the correct theory.

Lenin is absent from work, therefore we have to redouble our efforts, all together; all of us have with increased vigilance to protect the revolution from any danger that might threaten it; with increased determination we must use every opportunity for constructive work. And we shall do this, every one of us, from the member of the Central Committee to the non-party soldier of the Red Army.

Our labor is very slow, comrades. Although the scale of endeavor is vast, we proceed step by step, and the methods are very "prosaic": balance sheets and budgeting, taxes in kind and export of grain. All this proceeds tardily and we are constructing the edifice brick by brick . . . Is there not a danger that our party will degenerate into a petty catchpenny? We cannot tolerate this sort of degeneration any more than we can allow, even in the slightest degree, any split within the effective unity of the party. Even if the present state of affairs should be seriously prolonged, it will not, however, last forever. Perhaps it will not last very long at all.

A revolutionary upheaval on a grand scale, such as the beginning of a revolution in Europe, may come earlier than many of us now expect. One of the strategic lessons which Lenin had taught us has to be particularly firmly kept in mind, namely, what he called *the politics of great turning points*: today on the barricades, and tomorrow in the trough of the Third Duma; today a clarion call to a world revolution, to a worldwide October—and tomorrow negotiations with Kühlmann and Czernin and the signing of the shameful Brest Litovsk Peace. The circumstances have changed or we assess them differently—we march westward, on Warsaw. . . . We are forced to revise our view of the situation—and there is the Riga Peace Treaty which, as you all know, can also be called shameful . . .

Besides—there is stubborn everyday work, brick by brick—economy, cutting down expenses, verification. Do we need five telephone operators or would three suffice? And if so, do not employ five, because this will cost the *muzhik* some additional *poods* of grain which he will have to deliver! Such are the everyday commonplace details of work, but, look! Will not from the Ruhr come the flame of revolution? Will it find us debased, demoralized? No, comrades, we are not degenerating, but we are changing our methods and our procedures, and the revolutionary safeguarding of the party still remains our first and foremost preoccupation. We are learning the job of accountancy and, at the same time, we keep a look-out sharply toward the West and toward the East and events will not catch us napping. By purging and enlarging our proletarian base

. . . we are prepared to make a compromise with the peasantry and with the *petit bourgeois,* we are tolerating the NEP-men, but into our party we shall not admit either a *petit bourgeois* or an NEP-man; if need be, we shall burn them out of the party with sulfuric acid or red-hot iron. [Applause]

At the Twelfth Congress, which will be the first Congress since October without Vladimir Ilyich, one of the very few Congresses in the history of our party at which he will not be present, we shall tell ourselves, we shall deeply engrave on our memory the precept: Don't get ossified, remember the art of sharp turnings, maneuver, but don't become diverted; enter into short-term or even long-term alliances, but do not let your allies infiltrate the party, remain true to yourself, remain the spearhead of the world revolution. And when from the West comes the beating of drums—because it will come—then, although we may be up to our necks in calculations, balance sheets, and the NEP, we shall answer at once and without any hesitation: We are revolutionaries from head to foot, we have been and we shall remain revolutionaries to the very end. [Stormy applause, the whole audience stands up and applauds.]

7. *Lenin Is Dead*

Lenin is dead. Lenin is no more. Obscure laws by which the work of the blood vessels is ruled have put an end to this life. Medical science proved impotent to achieve what was so passionately desired, so passionately demanded, by millions of human hearts. Many were those who would have unhesitatingly given their own blood, to the last drop, to revive, to restore the arteries of the great leader, Lenin, Ilyich, the unique, the only one. No miracle happened where science proved helpless. Lenin is no more. These words fall upon our mind as heavily as a giant rock falls into the sea. Can one believe it? Can one make peace with this?

The workers of the whole world will refuse to resign themselves to this fact, for the enemy is still terribly strong, the road is still long and the great task, the greatest in history, is not yet completed. The working classes the world over need Lenin—he is needed as perhaps no other man was ever needed in history.

The second attack of illness, more severe than the first, lasted over ten months. The arterial system, according to the bitter expression of the doctors, kept "playing up." What cruel play with Lenin's life! One could expect an improvement, almost a full recovery; but catastrophe was to be expected too. We were all awaiting recovery, and instead, catastrophe came. The brain cells which control the breathing refused to function; the prodigious thought was destroyed.

Now Ilyich is no more. The party is orphaned; and so is the working class. It is this feeling that came before all others at the news of our teacher's, our leader's death.

How shall we go forward? Shall we keep to the road, shall we not go astray? For Lenin, comrades, is no longer with us.

Lenin is no more, but Leninism remains. What was immortal in Lenin—his teaching, his work, his method, his example—lives on in us, in the party which he founded, in the first workers' state he led and guided.

Our hearts are now so overcome with grief because we were all privileged by history which made us Lenin's contemporaries; we worked next to him, we were taught by him. Our party represents Leninism in action; our party, collectively, leads the working masses. In all of us there lives a small part of Lenin, and this is the best part of each one of us.

How shall we go forward? With the torch of Leninism in our hands.

Shall we find the way? With our party's collective mind, with our party's collective will, we shall find the way.

Tomorrow, and the day after, and in a week and in a month we shall still ask: Is Lenin no more? Because his death will for long continue to seem impossible, incredible, a terribly arbitrary deed of nature.

Let that same sharp stab which we feel, which our hearts will feel at the thought that Lenin is no more—let this pain become for each of us a reminder, a warning, a summons: You bear a greater responsibility now. Be worthy of the leader who taught you.

In grief, mourning, and sorrow we shall close our ranks and hearts, close them more firmly for the new battles ahead.

Comrades-brothers, Lenin is no longer with us. Farewell, Ilyich, farewell, our leader.

Tiflis, Railway Station
January 22, 1924

Index